The Right Jeans

Nick Hamilton

2QT Limited (Publishing)

First Edition published 2024 by
2QT Limited (Publishing)
United Kingdom

Copyright © Nick Hamilton

The right of Nick Hamilton to be identified as the author of this work has been asserted by him in accordance with the Copyright, Designs and Patents Act 1988

All rights reserved. This book is sold subject to the condition that no part of this book is to be reproduced, in any shape or form. Or by way of trade, stored in a retrieval system or transmitted in any form or by any means, electronic, mechanical, photocopying, recording, be lent, re-sold, hired out or otherwise circulated in any form of binding or cover other than that in which it is published and without a similar condition, including this condition being imposed on the subsequent purchaser, without prior permission of the copyright holder.

Publisher Disclaimer:
The events in this memoir are described according to the author's recollection; recognition and understanding of the events and individuals mentioned and are in no way intended to mislead or offend. As such the Publisher does not hold any responsibility for any inaccuracies or opinions expressed by the author. Every effort has been made to acknowledge and gain any permission from organisations and persons mentioned in this book. Any enquiries should be directed to the author.

Cover image: © Nick Hamilton

Printed by IngramSpark

A CIP catalogue record for this book is available from the British Library

ISBN 978-1-7385640-4-0

For Dad

Without whom I would only be half the man I am.

Biography

Nick Hamilton is a well-known horticultural expert, having trained at Writtle College before gaining experience at several wholesale nurseries before going into business with his dad at Barnsdale. They worked together for several years before Geoff's death, after which Nick took on Barnsdale Gardens and opened them to the public in 1997. They continue to inspire, educate and enthral the thousands of gardeners and non-gardeners who visit every year.

Nick is the author of *The Right Genes* and two organic gardening books, as well as writing for magazines and other publications. He has appeared on BBC2's *Gardeners' World* and several other television programmes and has regular gardening slots on BBC Radio Leicester and Rutland and Stamford Sound.

Preface

This is the second part of my trilogy about my dad, Geoffrey Stephen Hamilton, known to millions as just plain Geoff Hamilton, a television gardening superstar.

The filling of my three-part sandwich focuses on the seventeen years he spent in front of the BBC2 television cameras. In hindsight, I think that initially taking over the fruit-and-veg parts of the programme from Arthur Billett helped him enormously. Viewers were ready to be modernised in the way they grew these crops, and it seemed that Dad was just the man to take them on this journey.

He was definitely the breath of fresh air that *Gardeners' World* needed at this time of great transition in the way we gardened but also in the way we were starting to regard our gardens. It turned out that he was the right man in the right place at the right time to take the viewers along with him on this ride into the modern world.

He was a great encourager and educator both on and off the screen, taking pleasure in imparting his knowledge to improve the lives of others. He also knew how to phrase things or manipulate a situation to get the result he wanted in the nicest possible way without others realising what he was doing.

A fine example of this was making sure he gained an honest and critical opinion from a professional horticulturalist's viewpoint, namely me. I often get asked if I was forced to watch *Gardeners' World* every Friday night and my answer is always honest and always the same: yes, I did, but Dad never told me that I *had* to watch the programme. No, Dad was far craftier than that.

He would walk down to the nursery every Saturday morning and his opening line was always, 'Well, what did you think?' He knew that I needed to have an answer, and the only way I could do that was to watch the programme. I was in a situation where, if I was going to be out of the house at 8.30pm on a Friday night, I needed to present an absence note in advance just to avoid the inevitable question the following morning.

I am absolutely certain that his popularity was due to his character and his enthusiasm for what he did, and that this was very much moulded around his sense of humour, something he had inherited from his father Cyril. However, his success was primarily due to his ability to connect with his audience at the right level. This is an ability you are born with; it was not something Dad had learned, and I don't think it is something that you can be taught.

During my lifetime there have been a small number

of presenters who, in my opinion, have this quality; we can all identify them because they are the ones that we cannot turn off or switch channels from when they are on television. These are the people who captivate us and educate us without us knowing it is happening because we are enjoying their programme so much. Dad was definitely in that very select group.

This is the story of those seventeen years as I remember them from my perspective, as well as from stories Dad told me. I cannot guarantee that everything is completely true – but it does make for a good story all the same.

Chapter 1

It was never going to be particularly difficult because he'd done it all before. That very enjoyable year Dad had spent presenting *Gardening Diary* on Anglia Television had given him his first televisual experience, albeit to a regional and not a national audience. Now he was playing with the big boys on the most respected national television station in the world.

On the drive back to Barnsdale after his first guest appearance on BBC 2's *Gardeners' World*, it was all he could think about. The year he had spent fronting *Gardening Diary* had given him some of the experience he needed, but this was different. He had an inkling that this could be his opportunity to get onto television full time.

Passing on his extensive knowledge was something he loved to do and it excited him to think he could potentially do it to millions of keen gardeners.

His tutorial technique was very individual; it was not something he had learned but something he had been born with. It had been honed while dealing with customers at the Hamilton Garden Centre, when he was writing for *Garden News*, and had been put to best use in his current job as editor of *Practical Gardening* magazine. Under his tutelage the magazine readership had grown rapidly and subscriptions were at an all-time high, but the monthly readership of the magazine was still a drop in the ocean compared to the number of people who watched *Gardeners' World*.

In 1979, the *Gardeners' World* viewing figures were vastly superior to all gardening magazine reader numbers; however, compared with most of the other programmes made by the BBC, it was at the bottom end of the weekly viewing list.

It was the only gardening programme on television and had managed to increase its audience to an average of around one million viewers a week, a figure the BBC was very pleased with. The improvements in the programme and its increased audience could be put firmly at the door of its producer, John Kenyon. He had moved to *Gardeners' World* from the BBC weekly programme *Farming* and been given just one remit: to improve the viewing figures. He had achieved that in a relatively short space of time, but he was not done yet. He knew that he could take *Gardeners' World* to heights it had never been before and now he knew how he was going to do it.

Dad had just completed his first appearance on the programme and was supposed to be concentrating on his driving on this unfamiliar trip home. Instead he was only using half his brain because the other half was racing, visualising all the things he could do to inspire people through the medium of television if he was offered another couple of guest appearances.

It was an odd situation because I clearly remember that when I was taking my driving lessons he was unwavering in his view that everyone should concentrate one hundred percent on their driving when behind the wheel of a car. But he was excited about what the future held after this unexpected return to the television screens, so I suppose he wavered not on the road just in his head.

He had no recollection of most of the drive back; as he walked through the door of his cottage, all he could remember were the ideas filling his head. Unlike his mother, Dad was not worried about age; it was something he had no control over so he wasn't going to waste energy thinking about it. What he did know, however, was that he had reached the age where ideas could just as quickly vacate his mind as they arrived so he had the sense to write them all down in a notebook – even before he put the kettle on. The ideas were so good that they were more important than a cuppa! Then he put his pencil, pad and ideas to one side and contemplated a very successful day over a belated cup of strong tea.

The following morning, over breakfast and a coffee, he read through the list he had left on the kitchen table. He was surprised at the quality of some of those ideas and shocked at how great he thought one or two could potentially translate to television. He felt a strong urge to follow through, to strike while his iron was hot.

How could he go about it? Was it best to go to John Kenyon? He was, after all, the man who had given Dad the opportunity in the first place – but was he the man to go to with his ideas? Was he in tune with Dad, or should Dad go higher – maybe even to the top? The one major hurdle in this last thought was that he didn't know who 'the top' was. He was a BBC presenting virgin and had no idea of the structure of this vast corporation.

Obviously these days we would get out our phone, tablet or laptop and find most of this information in seconds on the internet but in 1979, hard as it is to believe, nobody had heard of the internet so the process was far harder.

Dad felt he had three options. He could ask John Kenyon who to approach, but if he did that then he would have burned his bridges if it turned out that John was the man to go to. He could contact the BBC directly and ask the receptionist who to approach – a good idea, but what if John got wind of it? He could ask a BBC employee but the only ones he knew worked on *Gardeners' World* and were definitely too close to home.

He decided to think carefully about it for a day or two; he was clear in his own mind that he would probably only get one shot at making his proposals.

Realising that all this contemplation had made him late leaving for work, he gulped down the last of his coffee and set off for the EMAP offices in Peterborough.

When he arrived, he set about finishing the main article to go into the July copy of *Practical Gardening*.

He was in full flow, banging away at the keys of his typewriter, and had written one-and-a-half paragraphs before he was abruptly interrupted by the phone. Not one to let a good idea pass, he let it ring until he got to the end of the sentence before picking up the receiver.

He wasn't in the best frame of mind; in fact, he was a bit annoyed because these interruptions had happened before. There were occasions when a tsunami of words in his head would pass down his arms to his fingertips and ultimately to the typewriter keys; the machine would glow red because of the speed his two index fingers banged out the words onto a sheet of crisp white paper. He had been writing articles long enough to know that usually, when this tsunami subsided, he would have almost exactly the number of words he needed. People phoning him when he was halfway through were not welcome because they tended to divert his text-laden tsunami to a place where it would become irretrievable. Even more irritatingly, he was heading towards an early lunch and the ringing phone would certainly put paid to that.

There were no answering machines at EMAP, so the phone must have rung at least seven times before Dad answered it. He was always polite, never wanting to let the person at the other end of the line know he was annoyed. Although he wasn't aware of it at the time, that politeness proved to be a great asset because this phone call was about to change his life. Forever.

The caller was always met with the same greeting: 'Hello, Geoff Hamilton'. This time what he really wanted to say was: 'I hope this is good because I've got all the words for a perfect article in my head and I was in full flow before you interrupted me.'

With hindsight, even if he'd said that no doubt this caller would have found it rather funny, particularly in the context of what he was about to ask.

'Hello, Geoff, it's John,' came the reply.

It was not a voice Dad recognised and he knew a lot of people called John, so that was no help in identifying the caller. His irritation grew. Just announcing 'John' was no good: it was one of the most common male names!

Not recognising the voice-name combination, Dad thought he'd just wing it and implemented his well-practiced response; he'd been in this situation many times on the phone and in person. 'Hello, John. How are you?' he said smoothly.

The pleasantries went on from there and the chit-chat lasted a couple of minutes, with Dad still blissfully unaware to whom he was talking. Was this someone he should know or a person he'd had a chance meeting with? Not knowing didn't lift Dad's mood but eventually, and much to his relief, the caller asked the question that revealed his identity.

If the National Lottery had been in existence at the time, to Dad that phone call would have been the winning ticket. The caller said these unforgettable words: 'Would you be able to come and do another guest appearance on *Gardeners' World*?'

The penny dropped. It was none other than John Kenyon – and he was keen for Dad to reappear on the programme.

How could he refuse? Quite obviously he couldn't, though he hoped that his reply did not give away his sheer joy at being asked.

He was told that this time he would need to go to Clacks Farm in Worcestershire, the home of Arthur Billet, one of the three regular presenters on *Gardeners' World*. This was great news. Dad didn't know Arthur, but that destination meant he would be assisting with something connected to fruit or veg. Arthur presented all the fruit-and-veg sections of the programme, and Clacks Farm was set out in a typically 1960s–70s' regimented style.

John said that he needed Dad for filming in a couple of weeks if he was free. Of course he was free – he would make sure he was free – but his answer was an understated, 'I'll have to double-check my diary, but yes, I think I can make that.' The sign of a man playing his cards very close to his chest!

There was no way that Dad was going to waste the next two weeks because he knew the value of being prepared. Every waking hour he wasn't working on his day job, he spent formulating a plan. In the evenings he sat at his kitchen table meticulously jotting down scenarios that would give him the opportunity to mention his list of fantastic ideas to John. Each morning, over breakfast, he read through them; this process of re-reading, after having slept on the ideas, generally resulted in a negative outcome that cancelled out a particular scenario. The following evening he would start again.

That was how important this opportunity was to Dad. After about ten days, and having filled his bin with scrunched-up jotting paper, he eventually felt that he had found a scenario that could – or *should* – work. The master plan had been hatched!

Dad was sure that if he could wangle the conversation round to the starting point he needed the rest would be easy, but even with an idea in the bag he didn't stop searching for something he may have forgotten to consider. However, nothing better came to him so he left Barnsdale with his proposals firmly implanted in his head and set off for Worcestershire.

He spent the journey reciting the script he had written to ensure that, if he got the chance to place his ideas at John Kenyon's feet, he could deliver it in a professional manner that befitted such an excellent plan.

When he arrived, he was relieved to be greeted by the same crew that he'd worked with so well just a couple of weeks earlier. They had seemed to like him as much as he liked them, and when John greeted him like a long-lost friend it only acted as fuel to Dad's fire and made him even more certain that his carefully constructed plan was about to come to fruition. He was most definitely a man on a mission and his confidence was growing by the second.

As the day progressed, filming went smoothly – a bit too smoothly really, because Dad finished his task in one take. It was a very professional performance and he was pleased because it would add credibility to his plan, but this early optimism dissipated as he realised how he had shot himself in the foot. He had finished all that had been asked of him and John was now busy in the editing suite checking over Dad's segment while the crew set up in another area to film Arthur.

Dad's performance had been perfect; he was no longer required and was free to go. John seemed keen to get on, and Dad realised that there was no time to talk to him. He said his goodbyes, got back in his car and set off home.

His appearance on *Gardeners' World* was a roaring success but in Dad's mind the day was a near-total disaster because he didn't get a chance to complete the most important task on the agenda that day – delivering his plan!

He mentally kicked himself all the way home for not managing to create an opening for his one-and-only chance to pitch his master plan to John; he felt that his chance of becoming a presenter on *Gardeners' World* was over. By the time he got home, he'd convinced himself to forget about forging a television career, focus on improving *Practical Gardening* magazine and forge an even more successful career as a gardening editor. If the world of television was not his destiny then he would put it out of his mind.

He was clear about this and set about making himself a well-deserved cup of tea after a long day travelling to and from Worcestershire. Dad was the sort of person who, when they decided on a course of action, would stick to it through thick and thin – whether he was right or not.

While he was sitting with his cup of tea, he found himself planning out the rest of his life – which involved no more television experiences. In horticulture we do a lot of planning for our efforts to come to fruition; we plan for vegetable rotation, sowing dates, follow-on crops and potential cropping dates. We don't just plan for our productive areas, we also plan the ornamental garden, even if this is just a scribble on a piece of paper. We tend to plan the design of our garden with bedding plants to fill in gaps and when to reproduce plants, with cuttings or sowing dates for those we propagate by seed. It's no wonder, then, that Dad found find himself planning his life, too.

By the time he had slurped the last of his tea, he had a new course of action in place. Surprisingly, the plan to forget about the television career had been unceremoniously hurled out of the window and replaced by a much better life plan. Uncharacteristically, he rigidly stuck to his original life plan for the length of time it took him to drink a cup of tea and then committed to the complete opposite! First thing in the morning, he would ring John Kenyon to talk to him about his plan.

Not wanting to come across as too keen, he waited until two minutes past nine the following morning before he called. Dad was hopeful that John was in his office at Pebble Mill, as that was the only telephone number he had for him. He was, and the buttering up started as soon as he'd said, 'Hello, John Kenyon.'

This time there was no way that Dad would be diverted from his course of action. He started by telling John how much he'd enjoyed the previous day's filming and how well he felt it went.

John was in total agreement and told Dad how the rest of the day had panned out. Although interesting, this was starting to divert Dad's focus and he knew that he needed to get back onto the plan. He was not going to be put off by idle chit-chat so he turned the conversation back to his own performance and the potential for taking it further.

The projects he hoped could be featured on *Gardeners' World* were on the desk in front of him. There were a lot of them and therefore a lot of explaining to do, but how should he approach this? Should he just start, plough through and risk John losing the will to live before he got to the end? Or should he cut and run?

Dad made a career-defining decision and changed his carefully crafted plan on the hoof by deciding not to tell John *any* of his ideas. He knew that it was a massive risk but it was one his head was telling him was worth taking.

He explained about the flood of ideas that he'd experienced on his drive back to Barnsdale and that there were just too many to go through over the phone; he needed to discuss them with John in person. Then he found himself blurting out, 'Have you ever been to Rutland?'

'No,' came the rather abrupt reply.

Undeterred, Dad continued. 'Would you like to come over for a weekend and I'll give you the grand tour of Barnsdale? We can talk about my ideas then.'

'Great,' came the equally short reply. The risk had paid off.

At Dad's behest, they arranged to meet the following weekend. On the Friday evening, John did something he had never done before: he crossed into Rutland. Following Dad's relatively accurate instructions, he found Barnsdale without any problems. Dad was pleased to be off the beaten track and away from populated areas, but it made first-time visiting all the harder.

Satisfied with a successful journey, John eased himself out of his car. As he turned to face Dad's cottage, directly in front of him stood a man with muddy knees, even muddier hands and a demented grin on his face: Dad.

Dad held out a muddy hand, fully expecting it to be met by one of John's, which it was, while managing a very hasty 'Hello, John', before unceremoniously bundling him into his Ford Granada. He didn't even wait for John to strap himself in, let alone unpack his weekend bag and have a relaxing cup of tea.

Dad started the engine, put his foot down firmly on the accelerator and hurtled off towards his local hostelry. John had been given no explanation so had no idea where this madman was taking him and why he was in such a rush.

It only took three minutes of almost supersonic speed for the Granada to get them to the Noel Arms in Whitwell; fortunately, no police were in the vicinity. Dad was on a mission and nothing would get in his way. He had his ideas to pitch to John and had found out that John was partial to real ale, something he'd let slip during their last filming session, so the pub was the perfect place to woo him.

The Noel Arms was Dad's local so Sam, the landlord, knew his tipple: Ruddles County Ale. Sam brought John a glass of it, too. Once John had sipped it and cast a pleased glance in Dad's direction, Sam continued to deliver John's new-found favourite ale every time his glass emptied over a period of several hours.

All through the evening, whilst Dad was in deep discussion with him, he didn't know how much of his ramblings John was taking in. It took Dad to well past closing time to convince him, but by the end of John's first experience of Rutland hospitality he had agreed that Dad should appear on *Gardeners' World* more regularly.

John woke the following morning with what could only be described politely as a bit of a headache; worse still, he had almost no recollection of the previous evening in the Noel Arms and consequently was confused as to why he had woken with such a pounding head. The only memories he had of the previous twelve hours were the harrowing drive to the pub and the three pints of Ruddles County Ale he had consumed. He was experienced in downing three pints of beer, so it shouldn't have affected him in such a way.

After a careful trip down the stairs, he found Dad at the kitchen table tucking into a stack of toast with a cup of piping hot coffee in hand. To John's dismay, he was as bright as a button.

Being the perfect host, Dad asked if he would like breakfast but all John needed was strong coffee. As he sipped at it, Dad rabbited on about all the things he felt were possible in their new working relationship. It took a while for the caffeine to kick in so John left him to it, feeling unable to comment until Dad had talked himself out.

John could not remember discussing *Gardeners' World* while they were in the pub or asking Dad if he would like to become a regular presenter. There was nothing in writing, so no contract had been made, which meant he could deny all knowledge and back out of the situation if need be. Legally he hadn't committed himself to anything as far as he was aware, although he was not quite sure why his brain was taking him down that route. Maybe it was still addled from the previous night's ale.

Some time later, John admitted to Dad that he'd spent

the journey from his home in Solihull to Barnsdale trying to think of ways to persuade Dad to appear on *Gardeners' World* more regularly. Dad was absolutely gutted by this revelation (which may seem odd as it was everything that he had hoped for) because he'd spent such time and effort creating his devious plan for his *Gardeners' World* coup and had been euphoric for days after because he thought he'd achieved his goal!

However, that was not the only reason Dad was devastated. It was not the time or effort he'd expended that was the real problem; all he could think about was the amount of good beer money he'd wasted plying John with Ruddles County Ale to get him to agree to something that John had wanted all along!

John Kenyon was a forward-looking producer and director, unquestionably the best that Dad worked with during his seventeen years on *Gardeners' World*. There were others that came close but none who matched him. It was during Dad's first guest appearance that John had seen the emergence of a great talent; he knew that if he could get Geoff Hamilton onto his presenting team, the programme would be all the better for it.

The thing he'd hoped for, but could not foresee, was how great *Gardeners' World* would become under his new presenter's tenure. It turned out that Dad was just the right person in just the right place at just the right time to take television gardening to its highest level.

Chapter Two

As the weeks passed Dad travelled to Clacks Farm for his *Gardeners' World* appearances, but there were a couple of occasions when they filmed at Barnsdale.

Dad had passed his long list of programme ideas to John before he had left Barnsdale after his ale-fuelled weekend visit, and John studied each idea, giving them the thought and attention they deserved. He was a smart chap and knew that virtually all the projects would make fantastic inserts into *Gardeners' World*, and he was also quick to understand that the majority needed to be prepared at Barnsdale prior to filming. There were veg that needed growing in situ, seeds to be sown, pricked out, potted on and grown on in the ground, as well as projects that would be followed over consecutive weeks.

This was the perfect opportunity for John to make a break from Clacks Farm and move the programme into a more modern era. He had known for some time that the layout of the site and the way Arthur Billet gardened had become 'old hat' and that viewers needed something different. He was certain that this was it and he began to travel to Rutland more and more frequently.

When Dad was a guest presenter on the programme at Clacks Farm, he didn't take much notice of the paraphernalia accompanying the crew and certainly had no idea how long filming took; he arrived in time for his segment and left when he'd finished. When the crew started to come to Barnsdale, John needed to ensure there was enough to film to make the journey worthwhile. This meant filming more than one section each time they came so John, his crew and everything that accompanied them entrenched themselves at Barnsdale for a full three days.

They usually arrived at the crack of dawn on Monday morning – well, that's what the crew called 9am. This suited Dad because he was more of a work-late-and-rise-later person. The crew would pull up Dad's relatively narrow driveway in their two very large outside broadcast lorries, followed by a handful of cars. Two lorries were required: one contained most of the equipment for filming, while the other contained the remaining equipment and the editing suite. This meant that everything they filmed at Barnsdale could be edited on site so John knew he had what he needed before he left at close of play on Wednesday afternoon.

These lorries were certainly not inconspicuous, being olive green with massive black letters on each side spelling out BBC. It was an odd scenario because the last thing John wanted was random Rutlanders turning up to watch the filming and disrupting the schedule, yet the lorries were so obvious when they drove up to Barnsdale.

Fortunately Dad had a row of large trees that separated the house from his two-acre productive area and this created a perfect screen for the lorries so they were hidden from the road. Although John was happy with this set up, if any keen *Gardeners' World* viewer really wanted to know where Barnsdale was and when they were filming, all they had to do was follow the lorries.

Happily, the inhabitants of Rutland were far too well-behaved and that never happened, though a couple of older ladies turned up one day to look at Dad's garden. It was not a filming day and they didn't seem bothered about that: they just wanted to see the garden they watched on television every Friday night.

Dad tried to explain to them that the garden was not open to visitors, but they were adamant that they had a right to go in. When he asked them why, they said they should be allowed in because they'd paid their television licence fee. They were not budging and Dad felt obliged to allow them something that, at the time, money couldn't buy: a trip around his garden

Once parked in their hidden location, the lorries stayed in situ for the full three days and the crew travelled back and forth to their lodgings in the cars. They were professionals and well-practised in the art of lorry unloading and setting up, so usually the filming day was ready to start at around 9.30am – around the time John had finished his pre-filming mug of Barnsdale coffee.

John knew that Dad would always be ready to roll

as soon as filming started because Dad had spent the weekend making sure all was in place and ready for a swift start.

While the crew were setting up tripods, attaching cameras and carrying out sound checks, John and Dad would go through the basic details of what they would film that morning. The finer details were dealt with when the production team had set up and John could relate better to the things Dad was telling him.

Unlike most modern-day filming, the crew used three cameras to ensure they got exactly the shots they wanted every time. One camera focussed on a close-up of the work being done, one on a wide shot and the third filmed a normal scene. The person responsible for sound had to deal with a boom microphone as well as personal microphones. The latter were obviously to record the voices of those present – generally just Dad – and created a very odd situation on cooler days.

On warm spring, summer and autumn days, Dad was usually in the garden in a shirt, sleeves rolled up and the microphone attached near a buttonhole. However, on cooler days he often wore a jumper or sweatshirt, but the sound person seemed keen to keep the microphone in the same place: on his shirt but covered with his sweater. To me, it always looked like Dad was suffering from a rather excitable nipple – in the centre of his chest!

The boom's job was to pick up general background sound, such as birds tweeting and the wind blowing, which apparently was just as important as the dialogue. Unsurprisingly, they weren't overly keen on picking up the noise of cars racing along a nearby road, and even less keen on the Royal Air Force Tornado jets circling overhead. These came from an RAF base in nearby Cottesmore and often caused problems in the early days. You could almost guarantee that towards the end of a long piece of filming, a jet would whizz overhead from out of nowhere. Such a loud noise could only mean one thing – it all had to be done again. The main problem with the jets stationed at Cottesmore was that they took off from the base and usually just circled a lot, which meant timing became all important. Not ideal.

As it was a training base for British, German and Italian pilots, the pilots took a circular route while they got used to handling the Tornado jets; when they felt sufficiently comfortable, they would graduate to flying over the North Sea and elsewhere. It always seemed a bit odd to me that if they made a mistake during their familiarisation flights and crashed, they could potentially annihilate many residents of Rutland; if they practised over the North Sea and something went wrong, the pilot ejecting and the plane crashing would only kill a few cod and maybe the odd jellyfish.

This circular training that incorporated the Barnsdale flypast was vital for our, and our allies, armed forces but it played no part in John's plans for filming at Barnsdale.

Noise interruptions days became the norm and the crew seemed to work around them, but a few weeks later after an incredibly noisy jet-related first day of filming, John had had enough: he needed to do something about it. Too much time and too much film were being taken up with retakes – and that cost money.

That evening, after eating in the hotel restaurant, he excused himself and left the rest of the crew in the bar while he went to his room to construct a plan of action. He had not got to his position at the BBC without possessing the art of negotiation and having an uncanny knack of being able to manipulate situations in his favour; he was a Yorkshireman, after all. He pulled on all his experience and, come the morning, he was ready.

John set off for Day Two of filming but, before he left the hotel, he browsed the telephone directory for the phone number of the RAF base at Cottesmore. When he arrived at Barnsdale, he burst into the kitchen, scrap of paper in hand.

Dad, who was sitting at his kitchen table as usual eating toast with a mug of coffee close by, wasn't expecting such a dramatic start to the day. When John asked if he could use the telephone, Dad nodded; he couldn't actually speak because seconds earlier he'd forced his last oversized piece of toast into his mouth.

The only number John had been able to find for the RAF base put him through to the main reception. After what seemed an age, and having spoken to a long chain of RAF personnel each of a more senior rank, he was finally put through to his target: the station commander. John was ready. He had his plan and was determined that, no matter how long it took, he wasn't getting off the phone until he got the deal he needed.

He had decided on a gentle, reasonable approach to start with but had other methods of persuasion as back-up if he needed them. He had even borrowed an Ordnance Survey map of the area from hotel reception in case he needed the coordinates of Barnsdale so he could suggest other flight paths for these jets. He had put all his eggs into one basket so the pressure was on; if his tactic of going straight to the top didn't work, he had nowhere else to go.

Having explained to the station commander who he was and how important this particular programme was to the BBC and to millions of gardeners across the UK, John reiterated the importance of the Corporation to the lives of everyone who inhabited this fair isle. After his opening speech, he felt he had exhausted the kudos of the BBC so it was time to go for the jugular.

He had a suggestion to make, one that he never thought would be accepted, but he knew that he needed to be diplomatic to stand any chance of a positive outcome. He had his Ordnance Survey map open and asked the station commander if they would mind moving their flying circle so that the jets no longer flew over Barnsdale. He even mentioned that he had the co-ordinates to hand if they were required.

He'd delivered his first-level approach, but had it worked? He waited for the inevitable rejection and steadied himself for cranking up to the next level.

There was a pause – rather a long pause – as the station commander considered his options and his reply. While he waited, John had an overwhelming feeling of what it must be like to be a criminal standing in the dock waiting for the judge to announce his verdict and the inevitable sentence for yet another misdemeanour.

Then the station commander spoke, his voice gentle, precise and his words delivered in perfect Queen's English. He repeated almost exactly what John had said, as if to reassure himself that this was indeed the favour being requested by this BBC upstart.

John braced himself for the answer, sure that it would be a definite no. He knew what a massive amount of reorganisation would be needed to alter a flight path that had been in place for decades and that it would be of no benefit to the RAF. The station commander had come across as a very nice man: could John bring himself to be pushier to such a decent chap and put him under more intense pressure?

The wait seemed interminable but finally the commander spoke as gently and precisely as before but sounding unexpectedly jolly, which took John completely by surprise. He uttered seven words: 'Yes, that is no problem at all.'

John was flabbergasted; he'd expected at least a bit of a battle to get what he wanted but this was as seamless and easy as could be. He had started the day tired, having expended a lot of energy working himself up for a confrontation with the RAF that had petered out with a whimper!

The station commander even offered to change the route of the jets before the crew returned to film two weeks later. John wondered whether to push for the move to be made immediately to make his next two days filming easier but decided to cut and run with the fantastic deal he'd been offered.

John returned the phone receiver to its holder and stood for a while to take in what had just happened before returning to the kitchen. Dad was still sitting at the table; as he turned his head, he was greeted by his producer coming through the door with a grin like a cat that had just got the biggest tub of cream.

When they returned to Barnsdale two weeks later, it was so quiet that John felt it was almost like he was filming on a desert island. You would never have known there was an RAF base only four miles away; for the whole three days, they experienced complete silence and not so much as a stray aircraft flew overhead. Much later Dad discovered the reasoning behind the station commander's concession to John's very cheeky request: his wife was an avid viewer of the programme!

Filming at Barnsdale became much more regular as Arthur Billet and his garden at Clacks Farm were phased out of the programme. Dad's productive area became the home for all the fruit-and-veg features that were needed each week.

He'd been filming for a few months in this fortnightly fashion and taken to it like a duck to water. It was easy to see that this was Dad's true calling; this really was what he'd been put on this planet to do. Gardeners all over the country loved his presenting style, his muddy jeans and, most importantly to Dad, the practical parts of the programme that came from Barnsdale. Under John's guidance, the Barnsdale inserts were now not just fruit and veg but had been extended to include ornamental plants and landscaping. Dad was on a roll!

The one thing he had not bargained for was that the wily old fox John Kenyon had plans for him and the first of these was about to be implemented. It had been an excellent morning of filming, with Dad reeling off the all the different tasks that needed completing in no time at all; in fact each took only one take, which seemed to be the norm for him.

He knew that this fine effort would result in an extended lunch break with time to relax properly, to sit and enjoy his usual bread and cheese served with a lovely strong mug of tea. Mind you, it wasn't just Dad who got this regal treatment at lunchtime; he wasn't daft, John was his boss and he knew on which side his bread was buttered – literally. John was invited into the kitchen for a much more civilised lunch than the remainder of the BBC film crew, who usually had their packed lunches outside in the front garden when the sun shone or in the empty outside broadcast lorry if it was raining. No freshly baked bread with a selection of classic English and French cheeses for them.

However, it wasn't all food and feet up in Dad's

kitchen. Although he and John talked about a wide range of topics, conversation invariably turned to that morning's filming and the filming yet to come. They both knew that in this relaxed setting, with little chance of interruption and no prying ears, they could talk candidly about what was on their mind and that generally resulted in that the afternoon's filming going without a hitch.

On this occasion John detected Dad's gratification about the morning's filming and his enthusiasm to get back out there. It was obvious how well the day was going and how great Dad felt about it, so John knew this was the perfect opportunity to implement the first part of his plan.

When the opportunity came for him to speak, he explained that although Dad's presenting style was just what the programme needed there were undoubtedly ways to improve it – not to change who he was, just to improve how his delivery.

Dad looked somewhat confused by this unexpected revelation, particularly as they'd been talking about something totally unrelated to *Gardeners' World* or television in general. Their chit-chat had been about how the plans to twin Whitwell with Paris were coming along from an initial conversation between Dad and some friends in the Noel Arms.

When John blurted out his revelation, Dad was stunned. Undeterred by his obvious confusion and lack of desire to pursue this line of conversation, John forged on. 'The thing is, Geoff,' he said, 'you need to get yourself a television.'

A television? What was he talking about? Why did Dad need a television? He didn't understand but decided to give John's statement the thought it deserved. He was still the editor of *Practical Gardening* magazine; working for the BBC and filming for three days on *Gardeners' World* every two weeks didn't pay enough for him to give up his editorship. Not only that, as a consequence of losing three days of *Practical Gardening* work, when Dad returned home from his EMAP office most evenings were dedicated to catching up with his workload. Mind you, in summer he always made use of the lighter evenings to get into the garden first, so would often burn the summer midnight oil in his home office tapping away on his typewriter. Maybe because working until midnight wasn't hard enough, he had also started writing gardening books; book writing seemed to come hand in hand with the television work.

When he relayed this, John didn't look overly moved by Dad's rambling condemnation of the 'you must get a television' idea so he continued. 'I always buy a daily paper to keep up with the news and I have a radio, so I'm up to date with what is happening in the UK and around the world. Why on earth do I need a television?' He felt he had put his position across in a firm but not aggressive manner and that John would understand the reasoning behind him not needing or wanting a television.

John waited until he was sure that Dad had finished rabbiting on. 'In order to improve as a presenter, Geoff, you need to watch *Gardeners' World* every Friday night as if you were a viewer. It's definitely not about changing the way you are. I would never want to do that.'

He took a deep breath and continued. 'It's about identifying the little things that you could improve on. By watching each programme, you will also have new ideas about things that could feature in other programmes. It's amazing how random ideas can be generated from completely unrelated sections of a programme, either by watching yourself or one of the other presenters. You will need help – you can't rely on generating these ideas all by yourself. As a presenter I think you're great, but I say all this from experience.'

Considered as John's explanation was, it was like water off a duck's back because Dad could still not see the point of getting a television. It was not that he was a technophobe, he just couldn't see how John's reasoning worked – and he certainly didn't want to invest in a television to watch himself. He decided to argue his point for a little while longer.

Dad liked a constructive argument or discussion; he liked the cut and thrust and always approached them in a non-aggressive or arrogant way. As far as he was concerned this was discussion at its best, so he continued until he knew he'd exhausted all possible counter reasons. Eventually he had to bow to John's greater knowledge and expertise: if the boss said that you need to get a television, in the end you get a television!

That weekend, Dad tootled off to the town's only electrical store, Knight's of Oakham, hopeful that they would not have what he intended to buy because he wanted the same type of television he'd bought for the family in the 1960s: a black-and-white one.

This had only been part of our family for a couple of years before Dad realised that it was laying idle for most of the day. His three young sons were spending all their waking hours playing outside, so why was he paying the licence fee for something that was hardly ever used? This thought came to him during one of his money-saving exercises and he started to think of all the things he could spend that licence-fee money on. His mind was made up: the television had to go, and it was quickly sold to a young family further down Wharf Road.

To be honest, we didn't notice it had gone until a few months later when Dad went out and purchased another second-hand black-and-white television. It turned out that he was having withdrawal symptoms from not being able to watch the evening news.

Things had moved on since those halcyon days in Wharf Road, Wormley when, in order to change channel, you actually had to get out of your chair and press a large, tube-like button with the force of a punch by Mohammed Ali's famous right hand. By the late 1970s it was possible to recline in comfort and gently push a button on this newfangled thing called a remote control, so there was no need to get up. Anyway, you couldn't get up even if you wanted to because the remote control was the size of a small house and literally pinned you in your seat!

This time, Dad had got it into his head that if he was going to have to buy a television then he would spend the least amount of money on it as he could. He was only going to use it to watch *Gardeners' World* each Friday night, and he also was of an age where he was more than capable of pushing himself out of his seat and walking the two paces to change the channel. His first goal was not achieved as Knight's had no black-and white televisions, but he still left the shop happy: he bought the cheapest colour television they had, which came with no remote control!

His rented cottage already had an aerial with a cable into the living room so all he had to do was push that in, pop the plug into a socket and he was ready to go. He never admitted it but I'm sure he tuned into the evening news every day that week before his Friday appointment with *Gardeners' World* arrived.

At 8.30pm on Friday, he was positioned in his seat with the television on, pen and pad on the table beside him. John's words were still ringing in his ears so he was ready for whatever epiphany was about to be revealed.

The opening music heralded the start of *Gardeners' World*. As he started to watch, Dad realised that this was the first time he'd seen himself on the programme and on a screen that was larger than those in the editing suite of the BBC lorry. He wanted not to be impressed, but he also worried that he might get too engrossed and miss the lightning-bolt moments that John had predicted.

At the end of the thirty-minute programme, not only had he seen things he that he wished he hadn't, annoyingly he also had several ideas written on his pad just as John had predicted.

Dad felt bad; in fact, he felt *really* bad. It was not that he hated the idea of John being right, it was mainly that he could not believe he himself could have been so terribly wrong.

As a horticulturalist you understand from the beginning of your career that you will never know everything; virtually every day is a learning day, so Dad was used to being told about new ideas or new ways of doing things. But being so wrong was not the worst of it; that was the embarrassment he felt for arguing his view so vehemently and questioning John's superior knowledge and experience of television. He should have known better.

To his credit, my dad was not one to shy away from admitting to his mistakes. As soon as the programme finished, he telephoned John to tell him how right he had been and to apologise for ever doubting him. He then uttered the words that two weeks previously he'd never thought he would have to say: 'I promise to watch the programme every Friday night from now on.' And he did.

Having endured the trial of watching himself for the first time in full colour, he did tweak a couple of things he didn't like about the way he presented, mainly simplifying some terms that he used. He thought his natural, down-to-earth style didn't need tweaking, something John wholeheartedly agreed with. The main benefit of Dad watching *Gardeners' World* every week, though, was his constant flow of ideas – it was costing him a fortune in jotter pads!

It was John who suffered the most, however, because each time he arrived at Barnsdale he was confronted with a long, long list of ideas for future programmes. Pleased as he was about this, the poor man did suffer for his art.

Filming was now a fortnightly experience and the lunchtime routine was quickly established. John was all for having a relaxing hour while consuming the bread and cheese offered to him in Dad's kitchen, but Dad was keen to talk about ideas for future programmes as well as ideas for the next segment of filming.

On one particular day he was in full flow about how he felt he should approach the main task of that afternoon's session, planting out his summer bedding plants, when there was a knock at the door. That stopped him in his tracks because he was not expecting – nor wanting – a visitor during a filming day and particularly not during his lunchtime commentary.

There was a brief moment when John looked quizzically at him and Dad returned John's look with a bemused one of his own. Who an earth could that be? Dad excused himself from the table and went to see who his unwanted guest was.

He opened the door to a well-dressed, slightly balding man who was sporting one of the most impressive moustaches Dad had ever seen. He didn't recognise him; he was sure he would have remembered such a monumental moustache. All he could think to say was, 'Can I help you?'

He received a totally unexpected reply. 'Geoff Hamilton,' the man said, nodding in Dad's general direction.

This was a first for Dad: he had never been recognised before and, for a split second he thought this man had spotted him as the new and rising star on *Gardeners' World*. In an excited and proud tone, he replied, 'Yes, that certainly is me.'

How had this person discovered where Dad lived because his address was never mentioned on television? He did not dwell on this rather worrying thought, instead choosing to prepare himself for the obvious praise this beautifully moustachioed man was about to spout.

What he wasn't expecting was, 'Hello Mr Hamilton, I'm your friendly television detector man.'

It was incredibly rare for Dad to be stuck for a retort but those nine words sent him into a state of shock. When he opened his mouth nothing came out, which was fortunate because he knew exactly where this conversation was going and he needed time to think.

Since the 1950s, when the Post Office (in cahoots with the BBC) first introduced the idea of the television detector van, they perpetuated the myth that these vans would find anyone who did not have a licence. The vans actually existed and people were paid to drive them around, making sure they were as visible as possible; however, even though the vans were real, there was no detecting equipment inside them. The BBC ensured that if someone was caught watching a television without a licence, they were informed that it was the television detector van that had caught them. They were heavily promoted wherever and whenever possible because the Corporation was keen to instil fear as a means of ensuring maximum revenue from the licence fee – and it worked.

Whenever a van appeared in an area of a city, a town or village – or even if there was just a rumour about one – the jungle telegraph would spring into action and those without a licence would turn off their televisions to make sure they were not emitting a signal. Others actually went to the lengths of disconnecting them and hiding the set, just in case. We all believed these vans were the real McCoy and Dad was no different from millions of other television owners: he fell for the scam hook, line and sinker.

Having partially recovered his composure after being confronted by someone who not only had a magnificent moustache but had turned out to be a television detector man rather than a fan of the programme, Dad's brain went into overdrive. He was now in 'how the hell do I get out of this' mode.

He needed time to think, so he asked the man why he had knocked on his door. Having already deduced that he probably was not a follower of *Gardeners' World* based on the fact that he did not know that Dad was Geoff Hamilton, there was not much else of a reason for doing so.

The man informed Dad that he had come to check Dad's television licence was in date. At that moment Dad recalled that he'd been so focused on buying the television, he'd completely forgotten that he also needed a licence to go with it. He must have been so overjoyed at spending so little on the cheapest television he could find that the thought had completely gone from his mind.

He was not deliberately trying to watch his television illegally but it was so long since he'd owned one that he'd overlooked the need for the licence; it was so ridiculous that someone employed by the BBC would forget to get a licence so surely this man would understand his forgetfulness?

The television detector man recited the lines he had no doubt been supplied with when he accepted the job at the Post Office: 'I have been driving around Exton in my detector van and I forgot to turn my equipment off when I had finished. As I turned onto the main road, I got a very strong signal from this property. On checking my records, I don't have you listed as having a television licence.'

Immediately Dad knew that it would take a superhuman effort to get out of this. He trusted his quick and inventive brain to come good, so to buy a bit more time he asked this chap if he was sure the signal was coming from his house. Dad knew the answer even before he asked the question because the nearest property was two hundred yards away!

After a pause to check his notebook, the detector man replied that it was definitely this property. He was confident that he had his man – and another feather in his Post Office cap.

Unfortunately, this detector man had not come across Dad before and had started counting his chickens before they had hatched. Dad was not giving up so easily and his inventive brain had just thrown him a lifeline.

'Come with me,' he said and headed towards a group of tall trees near to the house. As they walked to the rear of them, they caught sight of the first large, olive-green, outside broadcast lorry. The big black letters BBC were clearly visible.

Dad walked past the first lorry to the second one, stopped, opened the door and pointed inside. 'Have a look in here,' he said to his newfound friend. 'I think you'll find this is where your television signal was coming from.'

The man poked his head around the door and was confronted by the editing suite fitted out with more television screens than he'd ever wished to encounter in one go.

He stared for a while before extracting his head from the doorway and announcing that he must be on his way. Having perpetuated the myth of his detector van he couldn't let Dad into the real secret and that left him somewhat stumped.

He trotted towards his van, half-walking and half-running, and leapt into the driver's seat. Turning the ignition as he landed, he crunched into first gear and sped off. The van disappeared down the drive in a cloud of dust.

As he watched it disappear into the distance, Dad was overcome with a wave of relief and disbelief about what had just happened. Gathering himself, he returned to the kitchen.

As he came through the doorway, John noticed that Dad's usual outdoor, rosy glow had disappeared from his face to be replaced with a ghost-like facade. On being asked if he was feeling unwell, Dad couldn't bring himself say what had just happened because John was an employee of the BBC – the very company he had inadvertently been defrauding!

Dad knew that there were lots of general garden and close-up flower shots to be done first thing after lunch for which was not required, so he asked if he could pop into Oakham because he'd just remembered there was something very important he had to do. John had no objection; little did he realise that Dad popping out involved a quick dash to the main Post Office to purchase a colour-television licence.

When he returned, Dad's cheeks were flushed and rosy again; he was now legal and above board and could safely watch himself on the television without the fear of internment in a damp and dingy prison cell.

I was always aware that Dad had an appalling memory and this was the main problem with this misdemeanour. The trouble was that after legally watching *Gardeners' World* for the next year, he would probably find himself in the same position again when the television licence became due for renewal.

It wasn't that he had a bad memory because he didn't; the problem lay in the way his memory worked. Remembering all the usual things that are important to people like birthdays, anniversaries, Christmas and buying or renewing his television licence, car insurance, etc, was important to Dad, but they didn't seem to be a priority for his brain. His brain's priority was remembering plant names, sowing dates, planting distances, sowing depths and all things horticultural. It wasn't a situation that needed close analysis: all you need to understand was that Dad lived and breathed horticulture. It was his life – but inadvertently it seemed to interfere with the workings of his memory. It was not just his television licence he forgot more than once; he also forgot my birthday – twice!

I've never been a materialistic person, in fact I've always found greater pleasure in giving than receiving, so I never mentioned to Dad when he forgot one of the greatest days in history: the date of my birth. I assume he never realised because neither did he ever mention it!

Having also been in horticulture all my life, I can understand the failings of one's memory because our business is all-consuming and definitely more of a life choice than a job. However, there were other factors to take into consideration. I have a 'detached' birthday compared to my brothers whose birthdays are four days apart and only a month after Christmas. This meant that one present-giving event rolled into the next and, when combined with January being the quietest month for horticulture, Dad had no other distractions to confuse his memory.

My birthday, however, came three months after those of my brothers, which left plenty of time for water to flow under the bridge; it is also a far, far too busy month in horticulture to think of peripheral things like birthdays. Literally everything is happening: plants are bursting forth with fantastic fresh, brightly coloured growth while others are already flowering, so being in the garden is a vibrant and exciting time. For Dad there was the added excitement of the veg plot, which gave him no time to dwell on other things.

This was the dilemma Dad dealt with every year. Thrown into the mix was filming for *Gardeners' World*, writing for *Practical Gardening*, evening talks to groups and personal appearances, so it's easy to understand that sometimes he found it difficult juggling everything while trying to keep all his balls in the air. As if that weren't enough, to further complicate matters he wasn't the most organised person; he almost always found it more thrilling to wing it and most of the time it worked fine – but just occasionally it didn't.

A missed birthday was something that I didn't worry about at the time, and as I have aged I now understand exactly why he forgot it – twice. I forgot all about a dentist's appointment once and two days later, when I realised what I had done, I had a 'flash of the blindingly obvious'. It was clear that I'd been blessed with the same appalling memory as Dad, but I can't remember when this realisation hit me because my memory isn't good enough!

My forgotten birthdays faded into the distance when Dad peaked with the quality of his unusual Christmas presents. What made this such a surprise was that he really did not like Christmas shopping. It was not just Christmas shopping that he hated; he actually disliked all types of shopping, always carrying out this onerous task begrudgingly and, when possible, putting it off to another day. After he and Mum separated, his hatred of shopping resulted in some very interesting combinations on his dinner plate because all too often he concluded that it was better to use up what was in his fridge rather than going shopping for more.

He applied this philosophy to clothes' shopping, too – not that he kept his clothes in the fridge. He had the bare minimum he needed to function so, quite rightly, there was no need for spares.

In the past Mum had done virtually all the Christmas shopping for food and presents, although Dad was not a complete bystander because he was always a great source of inspiration about the type of presents to get for each of his three children. After they separated and Dad was cut adrift and all alone when it came to purchasing presents, the stream of great ideas was still flowing. This had to battle with the temptation not to go shopping that continued as close to Christmas as he could get. The long and the short of it was that he became a confirmed Christmas Eve shopper. Leaving it to the last minute meant that, come what may, he had to come home with something. The pressure was ramped up when you consider that he always went Christmas shopping after lunch, hopefully when the crowds had died down.

For the first couple of years this system worked well and he came home with roughly what he had set out to buy, but his luck had to run out at some point and it did – catastrophically. As usual at this time of year, his mind was focused on planning what would happen in his garden during the coming year so he hadn't taken any interest in the combination of dates and days for December. He waited for the newspaper, radio or television to tell him when he was close to Christmas Eve, which was his prompt to buy the presents.

If he were still alive today that would not have been problematic; there are enough shops open seven days a week for him to get something even at the last minute. But in the mid-1970s no shops traded on Sundays and, remarkable as this may seem to the younger generation, there wasn't the internet or smartphones to place order on!

Dad usually began his tried-and-tested run up to Christmas by writing a list in mid-December and filing it where it was easy to find on the shelf in the kitchen; it would stay there until just after lunch on Christmas Eve when the fearful shopping experience beckoned.

He woke on Sunday morning and, as was his ritual, had his breakfast and a strong coffee before driving into Oakham to get his Sunday paper. He then, as he always did, spent about an hour and a half reading the paper before venturing into his garden. This was what happened without fail every Sunday, a staunchly guarded ritual that relieved the pressures of the previous working week.

On this particular Sunday in December, he returned home, made himself comfortable in his favourite armchair and started reading the front page of his paper, which seemed very Christmas heavy to him bearing in mind there was still a week to go. It was particularly surprising as the broadsheet newspapers were usually much less exuberant about the run up to Christmas than the tabloids. His eyes turned towards the top of the front cover and the date: Sunday 24th December 1975. This date did not trigger anything in him and he returned to the article he was reading.

It took another three pages before, with absolutely no warning, it hit him: 24th December, Christmas Eve! All he could think of was that his relaxing and enjoyable afternoon in his garden was about to be replaced by the terror that was Christmas shopping. 'Oh B*LL**KS, it's Sunday, nothing is open!!!!!!!!!'

He deflated into his armchair, his newspaper across his knees no longer the most important thing on this Sunday morning. 'Now what do I do?'

His mind raced with the possibilities to retrieve this dire situation, but it didn't race for long because there was no potential to buy anything of any significance. Only newsagents and garden centres were allowed to open on a Sunday, and he was committed to dropping off Christmas presents for us boys at 2pm the following day, Christmas Day – but he had no presents! 'B*LL**KS!' It was always the word he turned to when in the direst of situations. I am not sure why or how, but I think just saying it comforted him a bit.

On that same Sunday I was helping Mum and my brothers to put up the Christmas decorations, oblivious to the trauma twenty-five miles away in deepest Rutland. The furthest thing from my mind was that all three of us were about to experience a replica of my 'no-present birthday'.

From a reasonably young age I had put a lot of thought into buying presents for birthdays and Christmas, always trying to get something different, although whenever I bought either of my brothers an

LP as a present my first objective was to get one I also liked so I could tape it before I wrapped it.

From before he and Mum had separated, every time I'd asked Dad what he would like for his birthday or Christmas the answer had always been the same: 'I've got everything I need so there's no need to get me anything.' These were the words from the greatest, brilliantly whacky but perfect, present buyer I had ever known. However, his ideas for presents tended to be last minute, just like his shopping, because it seemed that great ideas came to him when he was under the greatest pressure.

For me there was only one thing for it and that was to put my Hamilton genes to the test and try to buy him a funny but useful present, although my thought process started at least a week prior to the event. For his thirty-eighth birthday I got the predictable response to my question so he received a pension book holder which, as I told him, would be the perfect holder for his cheque book. I had been thorough and actually checked to make sure the cheque book would fit into it. Although he never used it, he told me that he greatly appreciated the thought that went into choosing it.

Dad did not have a washing machine so when his clothes needed washing he would bag them up and take them to his local laundrette. I used this as inspiration for his next birthday in August 1975. The laundrette trips became something of a legend in our family, primarily because of the variation between what he went with and what he came home with. He had no idea how he managed it – and we certainly did not know – but he managed to leave home with perfectly matching socks and return every time with odd socks. That may have just been the excuse he had invented for being caught wearing odd socks, but as I was a young spring chicken I had no reason to doubt his explanation. That year I went out and bought him three pairs of socks, mixed them up so that they were all odd and wrapped them up, hoping that when he returned from the laundrette they might be matching pairs.

It's safe to say that his face was much more smiley and pleased when he opened this present compared to the pension book holder – and a few months later I discovered how successful my innovative present buying had been because he actually used the socks.

As I got older and started to notice some of the ideas he had, I began to worry about the thought processes that got him from an initial seed of an idea to the end product. Sometimes there seemed to be no initial thought and no journey to a great end product; one Christmas he turned up with three socks: half the socks I had given him for his birthday – one from each mixed pair. This was our Christmas present, one each, and it had actually been a full two years in the making.

On the morning of Christmas Eve 1975, panicking at the thought of no shops being open, his brain worked overtime and quickly came up with a solution. Not only was this a life saver but it also meant he could get back to his Sunday ritual of reading the newspaper and spending the afternoon in the garden. His remembered that each time he needed to take his clothes to the laundrette he emptied the loose change from his pockets into his bedside cabinet drawer, expecting one day to need it. That day had come.

The following afternoon, at precisely 2.13pm (he was always late) our doorbell rang and there he stood at the door with what looked like a heavily laden Co-op carrier bag. He was not expecting or intending to come in as he and Mum were not on speaking terms; it was better for all of us to swap presents on the doorstep.

Excited, I opened the door with one hand whilst clutching Dad's present in the other. We swapped: I passed him his present (a big bottle of multi-vitamins ideal for the older gentleman) and he passed me one of the socks I had bought him just four months earlier filled with something extraordinarily heavy. Then it was Steve's turn to swap presents, followed finally by Chris. With all the presents exchanged, Dad wished us all a happy Christmas, got back into his car and headed home.

We had to wait until we'd returned to the living room and collapsed to the floor before we had a chance to peer into our heavyweight socks. They were full of hard cash – no notes, just lots and lots of coins. In an instant we were transported back to Christmases in Hertfordshire when the whole of Christmas day was geared around keeping us occupied, and therefore quiet and content.

We spent most of the afternoon counting the mass of mainly copper coins in each of our socks. The thing Dad obviously hadn't contemplated after his fantastic salvaging of his self-inflicted Christmas-present dilemma was that as he dropped each handful of coins into the sock it stretched, making even more room for coins. He had continued filling until there were no coins left in the drawer, but there was so no guarantee that each child would get the same value in their sock as the other two. He knew that we would each be happy with whatever we got, so all he did was fill each sock to approximately the same depth and hope for the best.

As it turned out I got just over £12, a fortune to a thirteen-year-old in 1975; amazingly, both my brothers got almost exactly the same, give or take a few pence. It was remarkable that such manic sock filling had given rise to such a uniform distribution of funds – and even more miraculous when you consider that Dad was usually not that good with money.

He returned on Boxing Day morning to collect us for a day with him in Rutland. So that he was replenished in the sock department, we had counted our money and placed it in more suitable containers so that we could immediately return three somewhat saggy socks.

When we went back to school after the Christmas holiday, all the talk was about what presents people had received. I found myself having to admit that my Dad had given me a sock, and YES it was just the one sock, and YES it was my main present! I knew the comedy value of telling friends the barest of facts surrounding the single sock I had received from Dad and I milked it as much as I could, although eventually I had to come clean.

Both the Christmas of 1975 and Dad's memory blips with my two forgotten birthdays go a long way to understanding how he could forget to buy a television licence for his newly purchased television. As he aged, he no longer had to rely on his appalling day-to day-memory because someone at one of the banks invented an aid to the ageing parent: direct debit!

Chapter Three

Filming at Barnsdale was going better than John Kenyon could ever have expected or hoped for, which confirmed that his professional opinion had been vindicated – not that it was something he had ever worried about in this case. Yes, he had indeed discovered a gardening star and the icing on this brand-new cake was that the weekly viewing figures for *Gardeners' World* started to rise.

He and Dad were working well as a team; it was definitely all about the team, because John was a team player and he knew that his tried and tested method would work with my dad. So, while the crew were setting up the equipment on their first day of filming at Barnsdale, John took Dad to one side to tell him all he needed to know about how they would work together. He did not take long because it was a relatively simple method.

All John said was, 'Now, Geoff, you are the gardening expert who knows what needs doing and how to do it, so I will rely on you to tell me. I am the television expert, who knows how it needs to be filmed so that it looks the best it can on television. Together we are going to make the best gardening television programme there has ever been.'

That was all Dad needed to hear; in fact, this brilliant television man was a great inspiration to him and he knew that he had fallen on his feet with a perfect scenario that could not get any better. Little did he know…

Before Dad joined *Gardeners' World*, there was a team of three presenters. John was keen to keep that structure, although the current team had been together for some time and its two longest-serving presenters were heading into their twilight years.

John knew he needed to start to find replacements for Geoffrey Smith and Clay Jones; although Dad had taken to his new presenting role like a duck to water, this was not going to be the case with everyone. There was no way John was going to throw them in at the deep end without trying them out first, so his plan was to take prospective presenter candidates and give them short, practical inserts in the programme to see how they coped and came across. There was no better place to do that than at Barnsdale.

For one of many new faces offered a trial, who shall remain nameless, their contribution to the programme was to plant spring-flowering bulbs. This was their first introduction to the *Gardeners' World* viewers and therefore their big moment.

A selection of bulbs was to be planted in one of the

borders of the front garden at Barnsdale and the plan was to film this job first thing on Monday morning. As you would expect from someone given the opportunity of a lifetime, the new presenter arrived at Barnsdale early – certainly before Dad had finished his breakfast – and what a stroke of luck that was. It meant that Dad had the opportunity to give them a guided tour of his little estate and, more importantly, try to quell their inevitable nerves. This was such an important day that he wanted to ensure they gave it their best shot. He had a lot of faith in their capabilities and felt that they were just what *Gardeners' World* needed.

Although he tried to calm their nerves, it didn't seem to work because this short segment of filming didn't go as well as anticipated. This should not have been such a surprise because it happened with most first-time presenters, but on that particular day John was not his usual calm self. He expressed his concern to Dad about whether the new person had what it took to be a presenter, but Dad advised him to persevere because he felt that they were going to turn out to be something special.

John and Dad had formed a great professional and personal bond, so John trusted Dad's view, took his advice and they plodded on. Before long the spring-bulb planting had been completed and then it was over to Dad to film the jobs for the week ahead. The team soon caught up the time they'd lost during the morning's shenanigans and wrapped up the day only ten minutes later than planned. John's trust in Dad's intuition was well-founded; in the blink of an eye, a new presenter had hit their stride, was appearing weekly on *Gardeners' World* and became an invaluable member of this new but very successful team.

Dad seemed to have a gift for spotting talent and was always keen to help where he could. At the time, a relatively unknown horticultural journalist also benefited from his foresight and benevolence. With the world of horticultural journalism being relatively small, everyone knew everyone else and Dad was friends with most of them.

This particular young, up-and-coming journalist was a chap called Alan Titchmarsh. During a meeting with Dad, he'd lamented the lack of opportunities in horticultural journalism and the difficulty in generating sufficient income from writing to provide for his young family. Alan was considering going back into a regular forty-hour-a-week job in horticulture where he would be guaranteed a regular wage and not have to worry about when the next writing job would appear.

Dad was horrified. Having read lots of Alan's work he knew what a talent he was, and there was no way that he could allow such talent to go to waste because horticulture would definitely be the worse for it. Being the editor of *Practical Gardening*, Dad was in a position to offer Alan some regular monthly writing.

They both knew the score. Alan was already writing for a competitor of *Practical Gardening* and in those days journalists only wrote for one monthly publication, which made earning a living difficult unless you could balance it with other paid work.

Being the editor of *Practical Gardening* and a seasoned horticultural journalist, Dad was also aware of this regulation. While Alan was reminding Dad about it, and therefore why he couldn't write for another magazine, Dad hit him with his somewhat innovative idea. He never shied away from pushing boundaries when he felt it was needed or from pushing back against bureaucracy and big business to do his bit for the little man.

The answer to the problem was quite clear: Alan would have to write for *Practical Gardening* under a pseudonym. Alan was not sure. Was this ethical? Was it legal? He didn't know and was concerned that if he took this generous offer and someone found out, he could end up losing all his writing work.

Dad had already thought of this because at times his brain worked at lightning-fast speed. He was unconcerned by Alan's doubts and asked, 'Who will ever know it's you if you are writing under a pseudonym? There is no real need to have a photograph to accompany each article as others do, so we'll just put a name. If I don't tell anyone and you don't tell anyone, nobody will ever find out.'

This seemed to calm Alan's fears and he tentatively agreed to Dad's proposal. Three months later, Tom Derwent was born and instantly became a big hit with the *Practical Gardening* readership, although nobody ever knew what he looked like – until now!

That help Dad gave to a struggling but talented journalist was just the sort of leg up that Alan needed. Mind you, I don't think that Dad could have ever realised what the Tom Derwent / Alan Titchmarsh combination would go on to achieve. The one thing that most people would think of was that if this little caper was discovered not only would Tom Derwent have lost his job but probably Dad, too. This was the mark of my father, the type of calculated risk he was prepared to take for the benefit of horticulture and to help a friend in need.

There was a time when it seemed that all his friends, acquaintances and even people he did not know were in need. One such person was Eric Robson, someone Dad had not encountered before. Many readers will recognise the name, not because they knew him as a sheep farmer but because for twenty-five years Eric was the host of BBC Radio 4's *Gardeners' Question Time*.

Dad first came across Eric when he was asked to take on the role of chairperson for this important gardening programme just before he was due to broadcast his first show on 20th February 1994. Eric was rightly excited at the prospect and looking forward to being the rudder that steered an iconic radio programme into the next millennium. However, the day after the previous programme was broadcast by his predecessor, the whole panel announced that they were leaving to go to Classic

FM where they would present a rival panel show called *Classic Gardening Forum*. This left Eric sitting in the main seat of *Gardeners' Question Time* but with no panel to accompany him. All he could see was his whole Radio 4 experience crumbling around him.

Fortunately for him, Dad always bought a daily newspaper and was now a television news watcher, so he was aware of this catastrophic event. He didn't find it hard to get hold of Eric's telephone number and gave him a few words that were a lifesaver – or at least a job saver for Eric.

Having worked for the BBC for some time, Dad was aware that if *Gardeners' Question Time* came off air it might never return; although this was a miniscule risk, it was not one he was prepared to take. Once he got through to Eric, he offered his services for free as a guest panellist until the BBC could muster another panel for Eric to take charge of.

It only took two weeks for the new panel to be assembled but for those two weeks – and for free – Dad fielded all the listeners' questions in his own inimitable way. Being a modest man, he never did add 'saviour of BBC *Gardeners' Question Time*' to his CV but Eric never forgot his incredible kindness and made a point of telling me so when I first appeared on the show.

Dad liked to help and he didn't reserve this assistance for friends and work colleagues; he was also keen to help me either with good parental advice (his definition) or by using his position as editor and television presenter.

The perfect example was when I had to apply for my second-ever job interview. I had already worked for a year; before starting my horticultural diploma at Writtle College, I had to have worked for at least a year in a professional horticultural environment and I'd done this at the Hoddesdon Horticultural Research Station in Hertfordshire.

This essential year of practical experience before starting my three-year sandwich course had been arranged by the college. The research station had taken students for either their pre-college year or sandwich year of work for a long time, so they were well used to being offered students from Writtle and knew what to expect from them. Consequently, my application and acceptance process was done via letter, with no requirement for a formal interview. I had no need for parental assistance.

Finding somewhere to work for the middle year of my course was a totally different experience. The college helped each student find a suitable placement mainly by giving out lists of companies that had taken on students in the past. We were told that some of these would probably be keen to have another student, but that couldn't be guaranteed.

I quickly scrolled down the list looking for a company producing ornamental plants, my preferred sector, although I was also keen to try different things so I was looking for a company that had a few strings to its bow. I found one: Darby Nursery Stock in Norfolk.

This wholesale company had been set up in the late sixties by two brothers, Francis and Hugh Darby, and focused on producing ornamental plants (Francis's domain), and soft-fruit plants (Hugh's passion). For me, the best thing about the plant-producing section was that they did everything from propagation right through to saleable plants, so I would gain insight into all areas of an ornamental-plant business. It was exactly what I was looking for so I wrote off to introduce myself and set the wheels in motion. They had taken students from Writtle in the past and I was hopeful my letter would receive a positive response.

My hopes were fulfilled. After receiving a cordial reply, I arranged an interview for 11am on Monday 4th July. Very excited, that weekend I tootled up to Barnsdale to tell Dad the good news.

He was ecstatic and suddenly keen to be involved. His level of enthusiasm took me by surprise; he was so keen that he decided he should drive me there himself. To him it was a perfect situation because he wasn't needed for filming on that day so I could stay at Barnsdale the night before and we could set off from there.

What could I say other than that would be great? He was so encouraging about my chosen career path that to have someone to talk to on the way would calm my nerves so I saw his offer as a positive thing.

Unexpectedly, his involvement started about three weeks before the interview during one of my regular visits. It was Saturday and he was busy on his veg plot preparing for the next BBC filming session on Monday, but this was not going to stop him helping.

His assistance came in the form of worldly parental advice based on his own experience and considered opinions. He must have been thinking about it for a while because I'd only just extricated myself from my car when he greeted me by asking how I was – and what was I wearing for my interview. No small talk, no waiting until we got inside and I was sitting with a fresh brew of tea, just straight to the question he needed answering.

Being a youngster and therefore inexperienced in the etiquette of the job interview, I'd planned to wear my best shirt (in fact my only good shirt), a jumper, a new pair of brown corduroy trousers and smart shoes (I also had only one pair of non-work footwear). Like Dad, I was not a follower of fashion so my wardrobe also consisted of the bare essentials. As I spent most of my life outside playing and working in mud, the need for interview-quality clothes was as close to nil as it could get.

Unfortunately Dad thought differently: he was 'old school' and wanted me to be all suited and booted. Him being obdurate in his stance was problematic but, to be fair, he'd known me since I was born and had to vigorously smack my bottom to get me out of my wilful, not-breathing mode and into breathing. Surely he must have realised that I was just like him – stubborn!

He knew I had listened to his advice and that I was

undecided about the way forward, but I agreed that I would seriously consider his idea.

I arrived at Barnsdale three weeks later for our trip into deepest, darkest Norfolk having sensibly left my interview clothes in the car. I went to find Dad. Unknown to him, I'd brought the only clothes I had at the time that were suitable for an interview, having decided in the intervening three weeks that my more modern, practical view on dressing for this interview was the better one.

This was greeted with a rather furrowed brow but, as I told Dad, I believed that they would be much more likely to employ someone who looked as if they didn't mind getting their hands dirty than someone who turned up in a suit for a job involving hands-on horticulture. Not only that, my corduroys were brand-spanking new! Was that not enough?

He still was far from convinced and at one point during our conversation I had a bit of a panic because I thought he was going to offer me his only suit to wear! But although my job at Darby Nursery Stock would not involve spending every day knee-deep in dirt, he understood what I meant and decided to do the parental thing and leave his son to find out the hard way.

The next day we set off on time – a very rare thing for Dad – and spent the journey talking mainly about his BBC schedule for the next day. I'd initiated this topic, one he was more than happy with, in case he wanted to return to the issue of interview clothing.

The conversation passed to and fro; before I knew it, we had pulled up outside the main offices of Darby Nursery Stock Limited. The business was split over two sites three miles apart. At the time, I didn't question how Dad knew which one to go to; I was oblivious to the obvious – that he had been there before.

Turning off the engine, he asked if I would like him to come in with me. I thought it was an odd request: to be accompanied into your interview by a parent holding your hand when you were twenty years of age? Then he mentioned casually that he knew Douglas Anderson, the managing director – the very managing director I'd been corresponding with and the one carrying out my interview!

I was, and still am, a pretty strong-willed soul and I was determined to get this job on my own merit. I politely declined Dad's offer, got out of the car and headed towards the office building.

When Mr Anderson greeted me, I deduced very quickly that he was Scottish – not difficult since his accent was so strong. I was still unaware what a lovely man he was, though. Having spent an enjoyable hour chatting, he took me around the propagation nursery site where I would be based if I were offered the job.

Mr Anderson was a decisive man who was obviously aware of the potential of the student standing in front of him. He thanked me for coming and told me that he would be pleased to offer me a position for my sandwich year. There was no, 'we'll let you know in due course'; he offered me the job there and then. Wanting to appear professional and decisive, I accepted immediately.

As I approached the car, my smile was so broad that there was no need for Dad to ask what had happened but he did so anyway. As we drove home, I excitedly filled him in with all the details. I also made sure to tell him that I was sure it was the corduroys that had swung it. I knew – and was fully aware that Dad knew too – that my little joke was nowhere near the truth, but I felt it necessary to make the point.

Trying to regain the higher ground over his middle son, Dad asked if Mr Anderson had mentioned him at all during my interview. That hadn't been on my mind at the time so I hadn't really noticed but, having been asked the question and thinking back, I struggled to remember his name coming up. I never did find out whether it was just that Mr Anderson was a very insightful man, or whether he felt no reason to mention Dad; at no point did he let on that he knew Dad personally apart from at the end of my interview. As we shook hands, he thanked me for coming and said how much he was looking forward to me starting work for them and asked me to pass on his best wishes to my father Geoff.

Throughout this whole process I had found Dad's advice helpful because he was experienced not just at being interviewed but also interviewing others; however, I think he also learned something because he never commented on my clothes again!

The trouble with parental advice is that you need to make sure that you are on rock-solid ground before dispensing it and, unfortunately for Dad, he was on quite soggy ground. Just like his unfashionable middle son he was always in his work clothes, so his insistence on giving interview-clothing advice seemed somewhat inappropriate. But things were about to get a whole lot worse: together with his co-presenter Clay Jones, Dad was about to be named as one member of the worst-dressed duo on television.

This accusation was first printed in the *Manchester Evening News* on 16th March 1982 in a letter written by Smarty Pants from Prestwich that featured in the *That's Entertainment: TV Postbag* section of the newspaper. Mr, Mrs, Ms, Miss or Master Smarty Pants – we never knew which it was – wanted to award a prize for the worst-dressed duo on TV: the presenters of *Gardeners' World*.

Neither Dad nor I could offer a defence against this accusation because Dad possessed what can only be described as an horrific waterproof coat. It was only seen on *Gardeners' World* when filming during inclement weather, but bearing in mind our British climate that meant it was seen far too often. He had bought it while working for *Garden News* some years before, so not only was it brown and orange (a popular combo in the late 1970s), it was also very well worn.

The coat was fine for wearing in your own garden where nobody could see you, but it certainly was not the sort you would wear in public, let alone sport in front of more than a million television viewers. Dad's partner in crime, Clay Jones, was vilified for wearing a plain brown anorak but, to be honest, that wasn't noticeable when he stood next to Dad's monstrosity. (At this point, I think it relevant to re-state that this was the man who made derisory comments about my very trendy brown corduroy trousers!)

If ever someone needed a nudge it was Dad and this was just the nudge he needed to make him take a second look at his coat, but he struggled to see a problem with it until he sought advice from friends and colleagues. Then he realised Smarty Pants had hit the nail right on the head.

Always humble, and never one to miss an opportunity, Dad replied to Smarty Pants in a letter that was included a few weeks later in the same section of the *Manchester Evening News* under the heading: *HERE'S ONE GARDENER WHO'S … Turning over a new leaf.*

It was a beautifully constructed headline by the newspaper's editor because Dad sent a photograph too. It showed him standing next to a compost bin, dressed in a three-piece dinner suit, holding a digging fork with his awful brown-and-orange coat hanging from the end of it over the compost bin. Fortunately for the readers, the picture was in black and white so the true horror of the jacket was suitably subdued. No health warning to readers was required.

Dad's letter apologised profusely to Smarty Pants for

the coat misdemeanour and promised to do better in future; in his tongue-in-cheek apology, he said he was only a humble gardener and not aware of the niceties of gardening haute couture.

Despite his apology, he couldn't bear to throw away a much-loved coat, however. Once the photograph had been taken, the coat was retrieved from the end of the fork and returned to its hook on the back of the kitchen door. Dad did concede that it could only be worn in the garden on non-filming days, and that continued until the sad day when it disintegrated to a point that it *had* to be disposed of.

The response Dad sent to the *Manchester Evening News* really hit the mark and clearly showed his sense of humour. There is no question that his personality was shaped by his terrible sense of humour and throughout his life it reared its ugly head more often than was sensible. It was genetic, passed down from his father Cyril's side of the family.

This created a problem for the unwitting BBC viewers because the reason Dad and John Kenyon got on so well was that they both had a similar terrible sense of humour. A classic example of this aired on *Gardeners' World* in the early 1980s when Dad decided it was a good time to show viewers how to sow seeds. As he was becoming known for his great budget ideas, he needed to find an economical method because this was something that was important to most viewers. Traditionally, gardeners are not wealthy people and for generations they've had to make do and mend. Gardeners could improvise with almost anything to achieve what they needed but they could not afford to buy. Dad was fully aware of the pride associated with this way of gardening, as he had done it himself.

Sowing seeds in the traditional way, by using a plastic or wooden seed tray purchased from his local garden centre, was out of the question so Dad decided to use a by-product of modern life: the takeaway food tray. He was filmed standing at his greenhouse potting bench and began by saying that he was going to sow seed but, instead of using the usual plastic or wooden seed tray, he would reuse something that most people had in their houses. At this point he produced his empty and clean aluminium Chinese takeaway tray.

He showed viewers how easy it was to make drainage holes in the base using his label-writing pencil, filled it with a seed-sowing compost and lightly firmed it with his home-made wooden compost firmer. After giving the tray a good water, he sprinkled lettuce seed lightly over the level surface and covered it with a thin layer of the same compost. He wrote the label, pushed it into one end of the tray and said that it could now be put into a propagator or onto a windowsill. Then he looked straight into the camera lens.

When I asked him, he swore what followed was not planned but had popped into his head at the time. He paused for just enough time for maximum impact then, still looking straight at the camera, said, 'The only problem with sowing into a Chinese takeaway tray is that once you've sown one, twenty minutes later you feel the urge to sow another.'

He smiled, satisfied with his little joke, and John Kenyon shouted, 'CUT!' Dad was like the cat that got the cream, so pleased and proud of his subtle, comedic brilliance.

Any reasonable person would assume that John would have asked him to do that last bit again but this time without the terrible Chinese takeaway reference, or at least he'd have removed the last sentence and cheesy smile during the editing process. But that would assume John was a conventional producer/director and he wasn't. Consequently, millions of viewers (including me) watched this terrible seed-sowing Chinese-takeaway joke unfold on *Gardeners' World* that Friday night. I'll never know how many viewers ended up in the same pose that I struck at the end of the joke: head in hands, mumbling, 'Oh no!'. I wondered if I could ever again admit to anyone that he was my dad. Either that or like-minded souls smiled along with him as they watched his comic genius and perfect timing reveal themselves on prime-time BBC television. My preferred belief was that his joke would pass by the millions of *Gardeners' World* viewers unnoticed and at least I wouldn't have to walk the streets with my head bowed in shame.

This venture into comedy played on my mind so the next time I visited Dad at Barnsdale I felt the need for a son–father chat so that I could put forward the case for the defence of the potentially fragile emotional state of his viewers and my fledgling reputation. He needed to understand that nobody – *nobody* – should make jokes about Chinese takeaway trays on television. I hoped that after my beautifully worded statement he would understand, but unfortunately I got the impression he still thought it had been very, very funny and that the real reason such a comedic situation never reared its head again was because the opportunity did not arise.

What made the filming days at Barnsdale so enjoyable was that not just Dad and John were blessed with a sense of humour; the whole crew loved filming there and jokes and pranks were a constant feature. It was a great environment in which they worked together and that undoubtedly contributed to the quality of the filming.

There were many days when filming was delayed by a ten-minute tea break just so the crew could get over the laughter generated by an occasional mistake or inadvertent inuendo from Dad. John quickly realised that a short break was the only way to clear heads – although sometimes things happened that warranted a complete break that lasted until the next day.

Such a delay had to be implemented after the Wisteria episode. Dad decided he wanted to include a feature on how to prune a Wisteria; not only was it was the right time of year, but he also had a rather unusual specimen for his demonstration. Usually Wisteria is seen as a climbing plant that grows against a nice sunny wall but Dad had been given a standard Wisteria, a variety producing beautiful flowers during May and June that had been grafted onto a straight, sturdy stem about 4ft (90cm) high. He was always very keen to show his viewers something unusual in order to broaden their knowledge; not only did this plant satisfy that requirement, it helped them to understand general pruning of a climbing Wisteria, too.

As was the belt-tightening norm for many large businesses at the time, the number of staff at the BBC had been trimmed. Now there was only a single camera rather than the usual three coming to Barnsdale, everything needed to be filmed more than once: a wide shot, one to show a general view, and a close-up. If each shot was required, then the insert had to be filmed three times; previously filming with three cameras had covered all bases so each job usually only needed doing once.

The slot for this particular item was a short one but there was still time to show how to prune and to show the finished plant. However, it wasn't long enough to show all that Dad felt was required, so he decided to prune the Wisteria shoots and leave just the last one to film. There was a method to his madness because he could then carry out his detailed explanation and, once the last shoot had been cut, there would be a perfect view of the finished plant. What foresight and what a great idea to save valuable filming time! Even though he was filming with a new producer/director, what could go wrong?

A plan was created, with the single camera shooting the general shot first, then the wide shot followed by the final close-up. Working with a single camera was new to Dad; this time he would have to pretend to prune the last remaining shoot twice and only complete the task when filming the final close-up shot, but he was happy to embrace this new way of working as part of an ever-changing job.

The camera was in place and, like a true professional, Dad went seamlessly through his explanation of how to prune a standard Wisteria. He must have been so overjoyed at cracking his dialogue in one go that when the producer/director shouted 'Cut!' he did!

The crew members looked at each other and then at Dad. The producer, who was reclining on the ground looking at the portable monitor screen, sat open-mouthed, unable to think of anything sensible to say. After what seemed like an eternity, he managed to whisper, 'Why did you cut it off?'

Still unaware of what he'd done, Dad replied, 'Because you told me to,' at which point the whole crew burst into hysterical laughter. Dad looked at the producer, who was ashen-faced and still sitting there not moving, and finally the penny dropped.

Unfortunately this was the only standard Wisteria at Barnsdale. With the last remaining shoot removed, filming the wide shot and close-up on the plant was now impossible. The producer was frantic. At the end of the previous week's broadcast, Dad had mentioned that next week they would show how to prune a standard Wisteria, so somehow it had to be done.

The producer decided on an early lunch so they could consider their options, which was a shrewd move because the cameraman still had the giggles and was in no fit state to hold a camera steady. The fact that his laugh was reminiscent of Muttley from the *Wacky Races* cartoon didn't help to calm the situation with the remainder of the crew.

Over lunch Dad thought of an alternative that managed to bring the blood back to the producer's face – it is amazing what bread and cheese can do. His idea was to film a close-up of the end of his secateurs cutting a shoot on the Wisteria climbing up and over his long pergola; being such a close-up, nobody would notice the difference between that and the standard one.

After lunch they put the plan into action. It turned out to be more problematic than they'd envisaged, not because it was hard to fake the shot they needed but because the crew couldn't forget the earlier experience. It took several attempts because of sporadic laugher from one crew member or another, and by this time even Dad was seeing the funny side of it.

Eventually this simple shot was completed and edited into the final sequence. As nobody ever mentioned any disparity in shoot size, Dad assumed they'd got away with one there, he noted this steep learning curve and accepted and embraced this new way of filming.

Chapter Four

Viewers of *Gardeners' World* were never aware of the lengths Dad went to in order to ensure they were bang up to date with the latest horticultural innovations. He was well aware of most gardeners' insatiable desire to find something new, so his job was to introduce his viewers to the newest available techniques and equipment. By doing this, he could guarantee that some of the Barnsdale slots on the programme were sprinkled with tasks, techniques or products that 99.9% of them had never seen before.

To guarantee this flow of new material, he avidly read every trade magazine or newspaper, scouring them from cover to cover, as well as visiting as many press events and trade shows as he could to look for that one little gem he could use. He liked to find something that professional horticulturalists were using – either a recently developed technique or a new tool – and modify it so that the amateur gardener could also be at the sharp end of modern horticulture.

Horticultural trade shows are no different to most trade shows: you are sent the show guide beforehand with the all-important list of exhibitors and what they will be exhibiting. Dad would peruse this at his leisure and select the most important companies or people to talk to so that when he arrived he knew exactly where to go and who to see.

He was always on the lookout for anyone or anything that he might have missed in the show guide as he mooched around. It often was not so much what the exhibitors had on their stands but more about what they didn't; he wanted to be there at the beginning of something new so he was keen to hear about ideas in the pipeline or things that were about to be released.

It was 1986 and the British Growers Look Ahead (BGLA) was imminent. Always an exciting time, this was the biggest and the 'must attend' show of the horticultural calendar, so large that it occupied several halls at the National Exhibition Centre in Birmingham. All the top horticultural industry suppliers were there but, unfortunately, this particular year Dad couldn't attend so his first deputy was deployed instead.

I was a twenty-four-year-old and dressed in the uniform of a young adult at the time: jeans, T-shirt, denim jacket and trainers. I arrived at the NEC clutching the list Dad had forced into my hand before I left, which had handy notes alongside each stand name and number detailing the information he needed or the request I should make on his behalf.

I learned a valuable life lesson that day, definitely one I wasn't expecting. As I wandered down the long aisles, I was surrounded by a vast range of horticultural products and services, each stand manned by one, two or more sales people, all of them looking for potential customers.

I quickly realised that I was not getting much attention from their scouring eyes, and when I did stop at a stand that was on Dad's list nobody seemed overly keen to talk to me. Always one to give people a second chance, I set myself a target of only being ignored or overlooked twice by the salespeople before I moved on. I wasn't going to tell them about the potential free television advertising they had just lost.

Being the age I was, and with minimal experience of the industry, I didn't have the confidence to talk horticulture in great depth with any of these 'experts' on their stands, so my plan was to mention who I was representing, grab their literature and run. There were a few occasions when there was no need to make any effort because a sales person came to chat with me the minute I walked onto their stand; that might have been because I was the only person on their stand at the time. Unsurprisingly, those who made the effort to acknowledge my presence showered me with material and information once I mentioned that I was representing Geoff Hamilton.

It was not that long since I'd been a student so I can understand that, to an overworked salesman, I probably looked like someone at college on the hunt for leaflets to help with their latest project. However, the lesson I learned that day was to never take people at face value because even as a student I was potentially a horticultural leader. They should have been keen to invest time in me if they wanted their company to have a long-term future.

I smiled a lot on my drive home as I thought about all those poor salespeople who had ignored me, unaware of what power I had clasped in my hand – the list from Dad. If nothing else, it just goes to show what gold a little bit of politeness can bring.

The following year Dad was back on the case and I was relieved of my BGLA duties so I could explore the show at my leisure. This was the year he found the product that would revolutionise his whole life. He had highlighted a company in his show guide that he hadn't heard of before that seemed to have a product he also hadn't heard of before. He returned home with one of the very first tubs of pelleted chicken manure ever produced. His excitement at this revolutionary discovery was palpable; he saw the massive potential for organic gardeners and couldn't wait to tell the world.

He knew that if he featured it on the following week's *Gardeners' World* he would be the first person to bring it to the public's attention. I can understand that, and why he was so excited to have found it, but I can't understand why he needed to remove the lid to show everyone this discovery just as dinner was being served in order to press home his point. A great organic fertiliser it may be, but it will never make it as an air freshener!

Dad was not just a man of great knowledge and passion, he was also a man with great foresight; nearly forty years later, this product is the mainstay of organic gardening as well as being used by non-organic gardeners. To be known as the man who brought pelleted chicken manure to the masses would be a perfect epitaph for Dad and one he would have been more than proud to have.

It wasn't just the new products and plants he showed viewers for which he will always be remembered, it was the adaptations he made to commercial horticulture practices and techniques. He was like a mad inventor and loads of thoughts, plans and prototypes were thrown by the wayside in order to find the one that really worked. He'd had plenty of practice making the toys and gadgets we wanted as children, as well as beds, chests of drawers, etc, so that there was no need to buy them. Why buy something when you can make something just as good for a fraction of the price was his philosophy in both his personal and professional life.

It was a strange mix that seemed to work: the centuries' old gardeners' tradition of making something out of nothing, known as 'make do and mend', merged with cutting-edge technology. There have been many times when I tried to follow his thought process from the original notion through to the finished product without success. More often than not, the trajectory of his thought seemed to have traversed a gaping canyon, which left the trail cold and me none the wiser. All I know is that the original thought was the seed that germinated, began to grow then burst into full bloom on our television screens with little or no apparent logic.

The perfect example of this was the obelisk he created for the Artisan's Cottage Garden, featured in *Geoff Hamilton's Cottage Gardens* series broadcast on BBC2. An obelisk is a great structure to have in the border for climbing plants to twine around because it brings an essential element of height. However, Dad knew that they could be pricey in a garden centre and their height and spread was usually standard because they were generally factory made; the range was limited, and that was all he needed to get his brain into gear.

He knew the importance of making something that fitted a space exactly as opposed to making do with what you can get, and he could show viewers how to make a beautiful, perfectly fitting obelisk at a fraction of the price of one in a garden centre. To push home the point, when anyone enquired he would tell them it only cost him £2.50 to make. That was not entirely true – it cost a bit more than that – but, made predominantly from roofing lathe, it was a lot cheaper than anything people could buy.

He created this masterpiece in an old stable that he'd turned into his workshop. It not only contained the woodworking tools he'd inherited from his dad Cyril but had the added bonus of a brick feeding trough, an essential if your woodwork involved using a horse. The problem was that the workshop was situated directly beneath Dad's office and only separated by a single layer of wooden floorboards. He had intended to insert some insulation but hadn't got round to it, which was a pity as that would have had the added bonus of partial soundproofing.

On a dull, rainy day in February, Dad decided to leave the jobs in the garden for a drier day and retreated to his workshop to start creating his new masterpiece. This meant that his office was free and, as I needed to research plants, I took the opportunity to make the most of the vast selection of books on his shelves. I was looking for specimens that would not only look good when planted in the new beds I'd created in the space around the nursery but would also act as propagating material.

I arrived with a cup of tea in one hand and jotter pad in the other, ready to create a list and planting sketch. From the start, it was difficult to concentrate: it was certainly not like researching in a library where nobody utters a word and you can hear a pin drop.

The silence was broken by constant sawing and a drill whirring. After a prolonged period of noise the drill stopped and I smiled, thinking Dad had finished whatever he was constructing and would tootle off for a well-earned cuppa. Then the hammering started. It got to the point where I was so distracted I could no longer absorb what I was reading; all I could think about was how he was managing to hammer for so long. The period of sawing and drilling in no way related to the period of hammering – but then it stopped and a brief moment of quiet followed.

That was shattered by some rather un-woodworker-like language: 'Bugger! Bugger! Bugger!' This outburst obviously meant that something was awry with whatever Dad was constructing. It was not the sort of language I would expect from a master woodworker – unless they were the frustrated utterings of the master-woodworker's apprentice!

Another brief silence followed. I wasn't sure whether to expect an escalation in the language or the hammering to recommence, but fortunately there were a few taps and then the drill started whirring as he bored into a piece of wood.

Just as I settled back into my research there was an exclamation that, if we'd had neighbours, they would definitely have heard: 'Oh buggerations!'

That was it: I could bear it no longer. My curiosity was at breaking point, so I put down my book and went to investigate. As I opened the door to the workshop all I saw was Dad's backside; he was bending over trying to attach something to a rather splendid looking obelisk.

My appearance seemed to spark something in him. He'd made the four sides of the obelisk and screwed them together before trying to attach the extra lattice work to the inside, but he had initially tried this from the outside in.

I was baffled by this cack-handed approach but only got two words into my question 'What are you trying to do?' when he announced exuberantly, 'I've got it!'

He didn't elaborate on what he'd got so I left him to it and returned to the office. After about forty-five minutes he appeared in the doorway to explain that the obvious answer was to take apart the four sides, attach the lattice work on the inside parts and then reassemble them. It had taken him over an hour of trying to attach these pieces of wood, including three 'buggers' and one 'buggerations', before he was struck with a flash of the blindingly obvious! I thought it was a nice touch when he painted the obelisk the same shade of blue he had turned the air in his workshop.

This left the finishing touch: a finial that would go on top of the obelisk. To link it with the rest of the garden, he thought a wooden acorn would do the job; he had used softwood acorn finials to finish off the tops of each of the fencing posts surrounding the Artisan's Cottage Garden.

Having made the obelisk so cheaply, he felt that he could push the boat out a bit and upgrade from softwood to hardwood. On paper that was a great idea but when he started to delve into the world of large, hardwood acorn finials he realised that the cheapest would be at least £25 – a full ten times more than he was telling people the whole obelisk had cost him to make.

That revelation made him feel a bit daft – he'd thought he could get one for less than £10 and had set his heart on it. Now he realised he could not bear to spend so much of his hard-earned cash on such an expensive, albeit stunning, finishing touch. There was no choice: he had to find an alternative solution.

As was often the case, in the face of adversity Dad came up trumps. This occasion was no different because it took him no time at all to find the perfect replacement to adorn the top of his masterpiece.

I have tried several times to understand the route his mind meandered along to get from the initial idea of an expensive hardwood finial to the end product, a toilet ballcock. Yes, a ballcock. What sane person would want to top something they were so proud of with part of a toilet? And it was not a meandering thought because it travelled like an Exocet missile. How could a normal person do that? That was my initial reaction, then it dawned on me why my own mind worked the way that it did – it was quite obviously Dad's fault!

Now that he'd decided what to do, he needed to action his plan. Arriving at our local builder's merchant, he was almost uncontrollably excited to find that a plastic ballcock would only cost him 79p. The whole 'make this for next to nothing' concept had just received the perfect finale (although one tiny fly in the ointment was the blue car-spray paint he had to buy to spray the ballcock the same colour as the main body of the obelisk and which cost twice as much as the ballcock did). Still, it did the job and he felt overwhelming satisfaction with his cheap substitute that now looked far more expensive than it was. It actually looked like a bona fide finial rather than a plastic ballcock stuck atop an obelisk.

For more years than I care to remember I've been happy to make that last statement to any visitor to Barnsdale Gardens. More than a million visitors have seen this obelisk and, without fail, those who didn't see the series or could not remember Dad making it had no idea it was finished off with a ballcock. He was so proud of his finished product, not just because it was better than he'd ever hoped for but because for months after the series aired he received so many letters, some with pictures, from viewers who had made their own. He was definitely flushed with success! (I'm sorry about that terrible pun, but I just couldn't resist!)

One of the first 'save yourself money' items he presented to his viewers early in his *Gardeners' World* career was his take on an alternative cold frame. He started as he meant to go on: it was free, having been snaffled from a pile of rubbish left behind once his local fruit-and-veg market had finished trading. It consisted of a box made from very thin slivers of wood (initially used to transport satsumas) that was ripe for modification. Dad used a scientific and well-thought-out approach, adapting it by attaching some baler twine as handles and a couple of onion bags to act as shading by laying them on the top, one bag to be used on average days and the extra one added on particularly bright, sunny days. The onion bags were snaffled from the same rubbish pile so they were also free. It was not just a basic cold frame; the baler twine handles meant that it could be moved to wherever it was required.

As time progressed, his creativity flourished from that small hillock of an idea with orange-box cold frame until he peaked at the summit of Mount Everest with his obelisk. This structure was the last of six that he created for one of the series he'd written and presented for the BBC. Geoff Hamilton's *Cottage Gardens* series was truly astonishing and set the benchmark for all the gardening programmes that followed, his own included.

This artisan's garden had been designed for a cottage gardener; traditionally they have very little money to spend on their gardens so home projects were definitely the way to go. Dad could indulge himself in his passion for creating and making – and if he could make it out of wood, all the better.

There was a thyme table with a bench, an idea he pinched from an original Dan Pearson design. This was basically a square wooden trough on four legs, filled with a soil, compost and grit mix before being planted with thymes. However, Dad always thought about the important things in life; if you managed to find time to sit on the bench, you definitely needed somewhere to put down your mug of tea. He placed some flat, water-worn slate between the thyme plants to act as natural coasters so that when you put down or picked up your mug you got a waft of thyme.

In the opposite corner of the garden, he hung his auricula theatre. This was a simple three-shelf contraption used to display potted auricula Primulas in the spring. Once the flowers had faded, they would be replaced with potted Pelargoniums that would be in full flower until the frosts. He made two hooks from strips of aluminium so that the theatre could be hung to give interest to any bare piece of fencing.

Around the corner from this he placed a tool chest that doubled as a potting bench, and a beehive compost bin. The tool chest was as practical as it was functional because it had a flap folded under the lid that could be used to level off the sloping lid. Once level, a home-made potting bench could be placed on it so that you were always working at the correct height.

The beehive compost bin was a stroke of genius and was not just functional but beautiful, too. He designed it to look like a genuine beehive so that it could be situated without being offensive to the eye as so many compost bins are. Usually compost bins are designed to be functional with no thought to their appearance, whereas this one was a balance between the two.

As the Artisan's Cottage Garden was only small everything needed to look just right, which was why Dad was so keen to make it all himself. Great thought went into the beehive's design: the lid and each section could be removed completely so that you would always be working at the right height and never strain your back when emptying the bin.

I always knew that his design was good – but did it work? Would people be convinced? Well, we generate mountains of compost in some of these bins so I know that works – and I definitely know that the look works, too. Now that we are open to the public, we regularly have people who refuse to go into the Artisan's Cottage Garden because they think it's an active beehive and they're frightened of insects that buzz!

Next to the beehive compost bin was an arbour seat. This was made from four fencing posts, some roofing lathe, feather-edge board and a plank of wood for the seat: a classic Barnsdale cheap and easy garden essential that you could make yourself. Dad reckoned that if someone could hold a saw at the right end and the right way up and move it backwards and forwards, they could make this seat because it was so simple, whereas the cold frame was slightly more involved.

He had included a couple of small beds for growing vegetables in his design for the Artisan's Cottage Garden. As most of the plants were to be self-raised, he felt a cold frame was an essential piece of kit. The design was not overly complicated, although it bore no similarity to his ultra-basic orange-box cold frame; if that was the basic model, this was definitely the Rolls-Royce of cold frames.

As was to be expected, it was blessed with the Geoff Hamilton touch. The cold frame was going to resemble the shape of a house with peaked end walls so that it could have an angled lid roof on each side. He knocked the base up easily and quickly – so easily and quickly that he didn't utter a single cross word – but he soon encountered a problem with the lid.

He had attached a central ridge close to the tip of each peak to which he planned to secure two hinged lids to give the desired roof effect. The lids would be made with a wooden frame encasing a sheet of Perspex, which was less dangerous than glass and easier to work with but still maximised the light. The only problem was that Perspex is much lighter than glass so each lid would need a hook to secure it to the base to prevent it blowing upwards and breaking off in the wind.

To Dad this was the perfect design but he was about to discover that it had a massive flaw. When he went to his local hardware store to buy the Perspex and the wood to make the surround, he was stunned to find the price of a sheet of it. There was absolutely no way he could use this material and still tell people it would be cheap to make, so he left the shop empty handed with his mind racing as he tried to think of an alternative.

He found that he was suffering from something he'd never experienced before. His flow of ideas had always resembled that of the Amazon river but now inventors' block had struck.

The cold frame was left to gather dust in the workshop for several days as he waited for the solution to pop into his head – and then he had a massive stroke of luck. He decided that the more he thought about it, the less likely it was that an idea would come to him but inspiration would strike if he got on with something else.

He got on with finishing the planting in the Artisan's Cottage Garden and this tried-and-tested method worked – though not in the way he expected. His first task was to fill his thyme table, so he needed to visit his local herb nursery in a small village seven miles away. During the drive he passed a cottage that was being renovated and glanced over to see what was happening. What caught his eye was a skip on the driveway and the window frame poking above its top. It was this that made him stop sharply: he had an idea.

Once he'd parked, he meandered over to the house and tried to get as close as he could to the skip to get a good look at the window frame without looking too suspicious. It was just what he wanted so he waited until he could attract the builder's attention. Needing to start his negotiation somewhere, he decided to go with the obvious question: 'Is that window frame being thrown away?' To be fair, it was in a skip which was a reasonable indication of its destination.

The builder's reply was an uninterested, 'Yes, mate.'

'How much do you want for it?' Dad asked. He thought he should indicate that he was willing to pay, even though his intention was to get it for free.

'You can take it for nothing,' the builder replied. 'It will make more space in the skip.'

Dad didn't need a second invitation and had the window out of the skip in a flash. Then he noticed a second window and, as he'd been given the all clear by the builder to remove anything he wanted, he took that one too.

Overjoyed with his two free windows, he continued

on his journey to the herb nursery and then back to Barnsdale to get straight onto finishing his construction.

Once the old paint had been rubbed down and both windows had received their white-gloss topcoat, they were ready for installing. Dad attached two hinges to each one and screwed them either side of his central cross bar. I watched him then do the obvious: he lifted each window up from the front and then put each one back down again to check that they worked. Unsurprisingly, they did.

Turning to me, he asked if I could get someone to help me carry it and pop it into position into the Artisan's Cottage Garden as he had other things to be getting on with.

There were two homemade handles, one at each end of the cold frame, to make moving it easier. I watched the programme featuring this garden essential and listened while he extolled the virtues of skip surfing (always with permission) and demonstrated how, when hinged, each window would open and close. He had attached a hook and eye to each one, in case the wind tried to blow them upwards, and painted the structure the same colour as the obelisk. With the two windows a bright, glossy white, it stood out – although there was really no need for it to stand out too much because at every opportunity he mentioned how great it was though only because he'd got his windows for free.

The one thing he omitted from his cold-frame exultations was that the windows were so well made and solid that when both of them were attached the whole thing weighed at least a tonne! I realised why the crafty old devil had not been keen to help move it!

As good as the cold frame was, it had a bit of a Frankenstein look and reminded me of the bridge he'd made several years before. This earlier concept was born from an initial, disheartening, age-related realisation.

Dad was an advocate of the raised-bed system for growing his vegetables and had created several in his two-acre plot at the original Barnsdale. As is standard, he'd constructed them so that they were 1.2m (4 ft) wide. He hadn't spent money on an expensive surround for his beds; instead the sides of each one was slightly sloped inwards to contain the soil. Between each bed he had left a pathway approximately 30cm (12 ins) wide to act not just as his route but also the point from which he worked. Anybody who is anybody knows that you should never set foot on your raised bed and must restrict yourself to treading on a pathway because one of the most important elements is preventing compaction. The idea is that you work to the middle of the bed from each pathway.

Dad was happy following these guidelines because he knew the resulting crops would be better for it as a result. The problem was that in order to maximise the use of his land he'd made his raised beds rather long and it took quite a while to walk up one side, across the top and back down the next pathway to work from the other side. It was obvious that it would be much easier (and save a whole load of time) if he leapt gazelle-like over the bed from one pathway to the opposite one.

We all encounter seminal moments that define where we are in our lives: the day we start school; the day we leave school; when we reach eighteen; when we reach twenty-one; getting married or finding our life partner; when a child is born. These are positive and very special moments in anyone's life but there are also seminal moments that we would be happier not experiencing. Dad was about to have one of those.

He was spending the afternoon planting lettuce into one of his raised beds and had completed each of the half rows on one side; the next step was to complete the other halves from the pathway on the other side. As he had done more times than he cared to remember, he began to coil, ready for his fluid leap over the bed, expecting to land like an Olympic gymnast on the opposite pathway. I never saw him raise his arms in the air and wait for the applause once he'd landed, but I'm pretty sure that was the feeling he had every time he did it!

He led with his right leg, eyes focused on the landing point in the centre of the opposite pathway but in mid-flight he suddenly and rather shockingly realised that he was not going to make it. He would have to put his right foot down on his beautifully cultivated bed, a disaster beyond disasters!

As his left foot landed on the path and his now-muddy right foot followed, he glanced back at the large footprint where his lettuce plants were about to be planted. Thinking on his feet, and hoping that nobody had seen his indiscretion, he quickly forked over the area to erase it and leave the bed as if nothing had happened.

He planted his lettuce, decided that was enough for the day because his heart was no longer in it and concluded that a drink would be the best way to ease his heavy spirits. It was while pouring the tonic on to rather too much gin that his thoughts turned from the negative to the positive. Suddenly his mind was racing and he was looking for a way to bridge the gap between the 1.2m bed and his diminishing athletic ability.

He managed to get a full two-thirds through his strong G&T before it dawned on him that to create a bridge between the two pathways what he needed was – a bridge!

The following morning he was in his workshop rummaging through the unused, leftover wood he had stored there. He had a picture in his head of what he wanted; it wouldn't be a complicated contraption but one he was sure would do the job admirably. He found what he was looking for, a strong and sturdy plank that would form the crossing part of the bridge, together with random offcuts to make a leg at each end.

When it was finished, it looked like a patchwork quilt; nothing matched, but then its sole purpose was to be functional rather than beautiful. He stood looking at his Heath Robinson construction admiringly until he realised that there was a bit of a snag: it was too long and heavy to lift from one end, so how would he move it up and down the bed?

Not to worry; within a few minutes he'd solved his dilemma and found a piece of thin rope that was perfect for creating a handle. He drilled a hole at each end of the bridge and knotted the rope. He tugged at it and lifted it fractionally off the ground before deciding that the only way to test it was to give it a trial run.

I have to admit that it was only in Dad's head that this was as exciting as the launching of the *Titanic* or England winning the World Cup in 1966, and he was definitely more excited than he should have been. He gently lowered the bridge down over the bed, hopped onto one end and tiptoed over to the other side before grabbing the rope, lifting it and moving the bridge a bit further down the bed. He repeated the procedure. Perfect: it worked better than he had hoped.

He was so pleased with his new invention that it was the first thing he showed me the next time I visited Barnsdale. In fact, it was not just a case of *showing* me, he made me have a go so that I could also enjoy the full experience and the pleasure that would follow.

There definitely was an epiphany on my part, but not necessarily the one Dad was hoping for. I was now standing in a pathway equidistant from each end of his long, raised beds, having nearly got a double hernia from moving his bridge, when I realised that it would be easier to walk up the pathway, across the top of the bed and back down the other path.

I told him so, but he was not interested in my evaluation of his most recent innovation and continued to use it, come what may. In fact, the only comment I got was that I was a 'spowpeen', a term he loved and one he used all my life when either I or one of my brothers failed in the strength department. I cannot find a reference to this word anywhere and can only assume that it was a malformation of the word 'spalpeen', which means 'someone who is a rascal'. It was probably used on him by his father.

Looking back at all the structures he made, it's clear that Dad liked to make things to last – but this also seemed to mean that he thought excessive weight would contribute to a long life!

Chapter Six

Dad's constructions, major or not, were often inspired by something he'd seen that triggered an idea that rattled around in his head for as long as it took for him to mould it into something usable. However, the garden designs he created had a much better pedigree; not only had Dad trained at Writtle College, he had also built gardens at the Royal Horticultural Society's Chelsea Flower Show.

Dad was a superb designer and landscaper, renowned in professional horticultural circles at the time for his expertise, so him being asked to construct gardens at the world's premier flower show was no surprise to his peers.

Even in his day job as a self-employed landscape gardener, he never left a job until it was finished to his very high standard, and there was no question that the Chelsea Flower Show would be any different. However, the main disparity was that if things did not go according to plan in his day job, he could take longer to finish even if he lost money doing so. With the Chelsea Flower Show, there were definite deadlines as to when you could start, when you finished and everything in between.

The garden had to be completely finished before judging day, which also happened to be press day; that was the day before the show opened to the general public, so there was absolutely no chance of being allowed to overrun.

Each year Dad worked fourteen-hour days to get the garden finished within the tight timescale. One of his garden builds was so elaborate and complex that he was still applying the finishing touches as the judges came into view. However stressful that particular garden build was, though, it was definitely not his most dramatic experience at the show.

The garden he was building for the 1965 Chelsea Flower Show started well and he thought he was at least half a day ahead of schedule; as anyone who has ever built a garden at this show will tell you, this is as rare as winning the football pools. He was in a happy place, but in the time it took him to finish his morning cup of tea things started to go rapidly downhill.

His delivery of paving slabs arrived, but when the van doors opened he realised to his horror that they had brought the wrong colour. He had no option but to send the van back to pick up the correct slabs. That put laying them back by at least a day and a half and would have a knock-on effect on the rest of his schedule. It was a disaster.

Then, as it tends to at some point every year during

the Chelsea Flower Show garden build, the rain started. Not only did it start, it continued unabated for days and Dad had to lay the slabs in far from ideal conditions. He would never have done it for a private customer but at least this paving only had to last a week before being ripped up again.

He worked like a Trojan to get the paving finished. It was the penultimate day and he had to get it done so that he could concentrate on completing his planting on the final build day.

As he worked, his eyes adjusted to the failing light and he had no idea of how dark it was getting. He had no time for unimportant deviations to his task, such as looking at his watch, until he had finished.

When he was done, he was very happy. The paving had been laid and, from what he could see of it bearing in mind that for the last hour he'd been working by moonlight, it looked perfect.

Now that he had a chance to look around, he realised how dark it was. He finally took the time to pull back his shirt sleeve, glanced at his watch and blinked in disbelief: it was nearly ten-thirty – no wonder it was dark! Even so, he was happy because he'd finally caught up with his schedule and now only had the planting on the last day, which he knew would be no problem. He already had all the plants that he needed on site so nothing else could go wrong.

While packing up his tools, he wondered why nobody from the RHS team had come to evict him at

9pm when the showground officially closed. For each of the previous build days, someone had been round at 8pm to remind him that he only had an hour left before he needed to leave the showground and the gates were locked. Then he remembered that earlier he'd had an unfortunate call of nature and that could have been the point when the timekeeper was doing their rounds. Maybe they'd visited his site and thought that he'd already gone.

He was pleased to have been missed because now the paving was finished and he had his positive vibe back for the final stretch. Happy with his day's work, he set off towards his usual exit point whistling a jolly tune.

When he eventually reached the Bull Ring Gate, two enormous wrought-iron structures, to his horror he found them closed and padlocked. To add to his woes, there was nobody around to let him out. Unperturbed, he decided to walk the full length of the showground to the only other exit, the Royal Hospital Entrance Gate, which was bound to be open.

He arrived to find these gates also firmly padlocked. That was it: he was well and truly locked in.

What was he to do now? He was not the type to panic but instead worked methodically through his options as he saw them. Should he bed down under cover in the marquee for the night? A good idea, but what would happen in the morning if he didn't wake in time and an unwary exhibitor stumbled across this sleeping beauty snoring next to their stand? He wasn't worried about the potential wrath of the RHS, more about the valuable time that would be wasted in getting his wrists slapped when he needed to finish planting his garden. Any time lost might result in him not finishing in time, so he dismissed that idea.

This narrowed his options down to one: scale these extraordinarily tall gates – but which would be easier to clamber over? While trying to decide without walking the length of the showground again to compare the height of the other set of gates, he realised that a worse fate might befall him if he were spotted clambering over a gate: he risked being arrested by a passing policeman who would inevitably confuse his attempt to break out of the showground with breaking in!

He realised there was no benefit in walking back to the Bull Ring Gates and decided to risk imprisonment by clambering over the obstacle in front of him, the Royal Hospital Entrance Gates. These were built to prevent illegal entry and had spear-like spikes at the top but, unperturbed, he clambered up and tentatively negotiated the spears before sliding down the other side. He was sure that nobody had spotted this manoeuvre. As there were no police sirens sounding, he was pretty sure that he'd got away with it.

The following morning when he arrived at the showground, nobody seemed any the wiser about his late-night exploits and there were no CCTV cameras to worry about in 1965. Dad tore into his work like a man possessed, determined to finish his last day of proper work on time and leave the showground legally while the gates were still open like all the other well-behaved boys and girls.

As he was the creator and builder of the show garden, the Royal Horticultural Society asked him to stay for press day. This event always took place on the Monday of show week, the day before the show officially opened, so that the press had full access to the site with no public to hinder them taking good photos; by giving access like this, the Society guaranteed the best media coverage. The same process occurs every year: the press want to fill the pages of their publication, while the objective of every exhibitor is to get a mention in a national publication.

For Dad it was also about getting contacts because the more members of the press he spoke to, the more they got to know each other and the more likely he would be to persuade them to write something about his creation. If his garden was mentioned he was likely to be name checked and that would definitely result in some designing and/or landscaping work coming his way.

Dad's mum, Rosa, was very proud of his involvement in the Chelsea Flower Show, not only because it was the premier flower show in the world but also because the posher members of society were in attendance. Even more important to Rosa was that members of the Royal Family visited on press day; being a keen gardener herself, it was usually the Queen who attended accompanied by Prince Phillip and other members of her family.

The combination of Dad attending on press day and the possibility of him meeting the Queen could be the event that capped Rosa's meteoric rise from working-class inner-London to the upper echelons of the middle-class Hertfordshire set. If she could attend the Chelsea Flower Show on a day when other posh people were not allowed in, that would be her crowning glory. She just had to be there!

Each year Dad worked at the flower show he could get a ticket for himself. This particular year, under extraordinary maternal pressure, he also managed to get his mum a ticket for press day. He knew that, if he was going to get her a ticket, she had to know about it at least two weeks prior to the event; this was the time Rosa needed to inform all her friends about her special day out, as well as buying herself a new hat – a special Chelsea Flower Show hat just in case the Queen passed within sight.

Both Dad and his father Cyril dreaded this build-up to the Chelsea Flower Show, and for Dad it was a bittersweet time. He loved everything about the show: the time spent building a garden; chatting to various members of the press and, if he got to stay during the show open days, talking to members of the public. However, if he managed to get Rosa a ticket for press day, the experience would be somewhat tainted. She would stand next to him for the whole day, resplendent in her more-than-special Chelsea Flower Show hat, trying to be a lot posher than she actually was. She wouldn't be able to contain herself when a member of the press stopped for a chat with Dad; on other occasions she had butted in to tell anyone and everyone who she was and how great her son was. Dad was embarrassed by what he saw as her over-egging his capabilities but he put up with it because he'd gain enough brownie points to see him through the rest of the year.

Most of the attendees on press day only saw the Queen from a distance because only a select few got to meet her. Unfortunately for Rosa, Dad was never one of them even though he was standing next to the woman wearing the poshest hat at the show, although Rosa was certain that her hat attracted some minor royals over to speak to him! She had a brush with royalty but did not manage to bag the biggest fish.

If Dad's experience of attending the Chelsea Flower Show press day with Rosa in tow was bad, Cyril's was considerably worse. He didn't have to attend on the day because Dad could only get one extra ticket so he was spared that, but he had to stand the cost of the posh hat bought from an expensive posh-hat shop.

Worse was to come. There was the inflated telephone bill that resulted from Rosa carrying out the vital task of phoning all her friends to tell them the news about her press ticket and 'meeting the Queen'. Her friends were blissfully unaware that 'meeting the Queen' was Rosa's term for glimpsing her from a distance.

It was fortunate that Cyril had stamina because for the following twelve months he had to endure listening to the same patter about his wife's experience at the flower show given to everyone Rosa deemed it necessary to maintain her perceived social position. This was the case for every function they attended and, unfortunately for Cyril, they attended a lot of functions!

I have a photograph of Dad meeting Princess Anne at the Chelsea Flower Show, but it was not one he showed to many people even though it had been professionally taken by a member of the gardening press. It is a black-and-white photo and she is standing directly in front of him with her mouth open, so she is obviously the one talking. Dad looks like a naughty child being told off by a parent although apparently – and we only have his word for it – this was not the case.

That was as far as he managed up the royal ladder so, in the end, Rosa had to be satisfied that any Royal is royal enough and she had photographic evidence of her family's connection to the Royal Family. More than adequate, she thought, to improve her standing in the Hertfordshire set.

Dad definitely had the 'gift of the gab', which was why anyone, regal or not, who stopped to talk to him had to be prised away. Mind you, this 'gift' for talking occasionally landed him in very hot water. Such an instance occurred on the day he popped down to see me at the nursery to tell me his good news. What occurred next opened my eyes to something I hadn't experienced before: the fascination many people have with celebrity.

Dad never referred to himself as a celebrity and never saw himself as anything more than a normal bloke doing his job. It was definitely not notoriety that attracted him, and he did not understand how being on television could make people view you so differently. Realistically he was in education, but unlike most other teachers his job was filmed for television. He looked and felt the same as he had done before he got the television job and so he behaved the same way he always had – but not everyone saw it like that.

Before Dad's arrival I was outside on the nursery talking about plants with a couple of ladies who looked to be in their late seventies. I hadn't been talking to them for long, just long enough to find out that they were looking for information about a particular conifer and might buy two if we had them.

Not wanting to let a sale slip through my fingers, I was explaining that this was a variety that I didn't grow but I had others that may be a good substitute; I had even started to run through a hastily thought up list. I had only got as far as the third alternative when I spotted Dad casually walking through the nursery entrance gate.

I was standing, as were the two ladies, sideways on to the gate so if I had spotted Dad out of the corner of my eye then so had they. Suddenly, in what can only be described as a very rude and unnecessary way while I was in mid-sentence, they simultaneously turned to face the approaching television gardening megastar and completely blanked me. I was left open-mouthed at such rudeness.

The lady who had just asked me the question repeated it to Dad. I was astounded because I had just told her that I did not grow the conifer she wanted. 'Ah Geoff, you will know,' she said.

The fact was that he didn't know. He was aware of many plants I grew because many of them had been propagated from his garden, but he was not aware of everything grown on the nursery and certainly had no idea of stock levels. Why should he have? But, as always, he was keen to be polite, attentive and above all amusing to what he quickly assessed were a couple of avid *Gardeners' World* viewers.

His response was a very jolly, 'Yes, ladies, what can I do for you?'

The lady taking the lead replied, 'I was looking for two Elwood's Gold conifers and wondered if you had some on the nursery?'

For those of you who are not familiar with this plant, their full name is Chamaecyparis lawsoniana 'Elwood's Gold', and they are classed as a slow-growing or dwarf conifer with golden-green foliage, tipped with gold.

Dad's reply was swift and witty (to him) and delivered with a beaming smile. 'What do you want those bloody horrible things for?'

Neither lady cracked a smile. The interrogator kept a straight face when she replied, 'I want them to go either side of my husband's gravestone.'

When a parent so effortlessly and rapidly manages to dig themselves a hole the size of a bomb crater, what can a caring and loving son do? Just like Dad, and with a beaming smile on my face, I waved and told him that I would see him later then disappeared back into the depths of our small nursery.

It was a good ten minutes before he re-appeared looking rather drained and no longer smiling. I, however, was grinning from ear to ear; due to the time it had taken, I knew how hard he must have worked to turn around the situation.

I asked him whether he had managed to dig himself out of the hole he'd dug. 'Just about, I think,' was his short, now-smiley reply. The smile was an indication that he had left two happy ladies; better still, he had persuaded them to have one of the alternatives I had already mentioned. The gravestone *faux pas* was never mentioned again.

Because the hole digging that Dad had performed, followed by his heroic repair of the situation, he almost forgot to tell me his wonderful news and the reason he had come to see me. The BBC had finally accepted his pitch for *Geoff Hamilton's Cottage Gardens* as a series of six half-hour programmes.

As I had just experienced, he could usually talk himself out of any situation, but this was not the real gift he was born with; that was the connection he could make with people whether face to face or through a television screen on *Gardeners' World*.

Being able to enthuse people is not only about putting words in the correct order and saying them at the right time, it is more about the way they are communicated. Dad was such a good communicator, which made the television job easy because all he had to do was stand in front of a camera and be himself. It was a fortunate but rocky road that had got him to this point, but he was more than happy to 'gift' this part of himself to the nation's gardeners. And yes, just as he was on television, in real life he was just as enthusiastic about horticulture.

I am in no doubt that he believed his life-long mission was to get as many people as possible who were not already gardening to give it a go, and for those who were to get much more out of their hobby. However, he never saw himself as a television star, a celebrity, a personality, or any other term used to elevate people who appear on television into something they are not; he only ever saw himself just like you or me – a normal bloke doing a job he loved. He would often become embarrassed when given special treatment and actively avoided anything that came remotely close to 'celebrity' whenever possible.

Such an occasion was the *Radio Times* Front Covers' Party, something he had not heard of before. This annual event was hosted by the BBC in London, and he received an invitation because he had appeared on the front cover of the magazine. It was an exclusive event as only the people who had appeared on a front cover in that particular year were invited. I say 'only the people' who had appeared but there was an exception: the top BBC brass also attended.

Dad knew it would definitely be one of those occasions he would love to miss, but in equal measure he felt obliged to attend. Like a child at school who hated PE and did not want to take part, it was almost as if he would need to provide a note from his parents to be allowed to miss the party. His presence was expected and the only acceptable excuse was death. Well, that was the way he explained it to me.

That left him in a bit of a pickle and unsure what to do. One half of his brain was telling him that to attend would be hell on earth, whilst the other half was eulogising the potential benefits an appearance could make to his BBC career. After agonising for some days, he came to what he deemed was the only acceptable conclusion: he would attend the party but arrive fashionably late in the hope that the BBC top brass were already there because then he would only have to stay for about forty-five minutes before making a discreet exit. This was not a figure plucked out of the air, it had been meticulously calculated using a pencil and the back of an old envelope; within forty-five-minutes period he believed he could catch the attention of the top BBC people.

His master plan involved the briefest conversations before he could get away with; if he did not get to speak to them, he would make eye contact with those on his list of 'important people'. Once he had mentally ticked off each person, he could slope off and hurtle back up the A1 to Rutland to the safety of celebrity-free Barnsdale. He was pleased with his finely tuned plan that, to him, seemed the perfect compromise.

On the day of the party he set off with his cunning plan embedded in his brain. The plan ran smoother than a Rolls-Royce engine and he seemed to be back at Barnsdale in no time at all, having managed to sneak in and out in less than his allotted forty-five minutes.

The same could be said for his attendance a year later. Although it was a long way to travel for less than three-quarters of an hour, he reassured himself that he'd made an important contribution to his burgeoning BBC career. As he later found out, it had also ticked all the BBC boxes – and the BBC do like their boxes well and truly ticked.

Returning from his second forty-five-minute attendance, he was sure that after appearing on the front cover of the *Radio Times* in two consecutive years, they would leave him alone for a bit. However, his continued success meant that the magazine staff were knocking down his door again for yet another front cover. This turned out to be his third and final appearance in 1994, but much to his horror they wanted him dressed up like a 1960s' pop star.

That was bad enough but the horrific photo shoot was followed by the dreaded Front Covers Party invitation later in the year. He was ready; his tried-and-tested formula had worked perfectly twice before and there was no reason why it shouldn't work again.

On the day of the party he followed his usual route: driving to High Barnet, parking his car and taking the tube train in to Euston Station. This was his preferred method as it saved time and the mayhem of dealing with the central London traffic.

Arriving at the BBC, he smiled from ear to ear because his timing was perfect. As far as he could see, the room was teeming with all the right people; this was exactly what he'd hoped for because, while travelling, he had decided that this time he wanted to be gone in a record-breaking thirty minutes. It wouldn't be easy but he was a determined man; once he had made his mind up there was no swaying him from his goal.

This left no time for idle chit-chat. Having slipped in unnoticed by what he considered the peripheral guests, he made a beeline for the people he needed to talk to. He ticked them off at a much faster rate than he had allocated for each one until he got to his final suited BBC executive, after which he glanced at his watch. Twenty minutes? Had the watch stopped or had he just achieved the impossible? He glanced again, trying not to make it too obvious. Yes, it was twenty minutes! Fantastic! Job done.

But then his mind started to play tricks. Had he managed to speak for such a short length of time with each person because his popularity amongst the powers-that-be was waning and they were no longer interested in talking to him? Surely that couldn't be so! He beat the demons in his head into submission and headed for the exit, sure that he was still in favour and it was just a record-breaking effort by Geoffrey Hamilton.

He looked at the floor as he headed for the door, determined not to catch anyone's eye for fear of having to stop and speak, which would hold him up and impact on his escape and his time of arrival back at Barnsdale.

He had done magnificently well; the exit door was now in front of him and he had encountered no hold-ups but, as his outstretched hand grasped the door handle, he was stopped in his tracks by someone calling out his name.

'Geoff, Geoff Hamilton,' boomed across the room. It was a voice he recognised but, being so focused on escape, at that precise moment he couldn't put a name or a face to the voice. Reluctantly he turned – and in a nanosecond this potentially horror-filled moment turned into something he knew would be an absolute pleasure.

Bounding towards him with his arm outstretched and ready for a handshake was Paul Merton. Dad raised his hand, which was grasped and shaken vigorously. 'Hello, Geoff,' Mr Merton said. 'Before you leave, I just wanted to let you know how much my wife enjoys *Gardeners' World*. She thinks you're absolutely great and particularly loves the stuff you do from Barnsdale.' At the time Paul Merton was married to Caroline Quentin, who was obviously the passionate gardener of the two.

All Dad could muster as a reply was, 'Thanks very much,' which, given his time again, would not have been the words he'd have chosen. For a man who was never short of something to say, it wasn't his greatest moment. Paul Merton turned and returned to the party while Dad went in the opposite direction, opened the door and made an unassuming exit.

He metaphorically kicked himself all the way home because he'd always been a great fan of Paul Merton. Now, given his moment, he'd been a little in awe of the man in front of him and that had seemed to render him incapable of sensible speech. He felt awkward that he was the one who had received plaudits when, deep down, he really wanted to return them. He wanted to be witty and entertaining, but all that came out were those pathetic three words.

For the rest of the short time he had left on this planet, Dad regretted both his mumbled reply and not taking the opportunity to let Paul Merton know how much pleasure he'd given him over the years. In hindsight, meeting the star if only for the briefest of moments had been more than enough reward for having to dress in an appalling bright-yellow shirt and don round, red sunglasses for the *Radio Times* front cover he had graced in August 1994.

For a man who was not a party animal, Dad attended a surprising number of BBC parties. The problem with all these other BBC parties was that they were impossible for him to avoid – because they were always held at Barnsdale.

Every year, on the last day of filming for a season of *Gardeners' World*, there would be an end-of-series' party in his barn. It was the prefect venue; it could accommodate the whole crew if the weather was bad, but if the sun shone there was a lovely, grassed area just outside.

The term 'BBC party' has to be used loosely because the venue, food and drink were provided by Dad and not the Corporation. Rutland has a plethora of great places for food and venues for parties but, of course, the BBC would have had to pay for those! I suppose Dad wasn't really in a position to complain because he'd started this ritual as a celebration of yet another successful series and a thank you to all the crew members for their contribution to the programme's success.

It wasn't just the crew that attended; the party was enhanced by the attendance of a BBC executive who generally appeared on the day and with no invitation. It was always the same man who came and each time he insisted on giving his corporate BBC thank-you speech. As he was slightly lacking in the height department, he liked to stand on a chair to make sure he could be seen and heard. There was no question that it was the bit of the party that the whole crew looked forward to the least, although they knew there was no getting away from it.

Once he was well above eye level, the executive would deliver his words very eloquently, prompted by the scrap of paper in his left hand. Although it was the same person each year it was not exactly the same speech, although they were quite similar bearing in mind the reason they had all congregated there.

He always started by thanking the crew for their input and the producer/director for their mastery at producing a wonderful programme. When thanking Dad for his contribution, he often referred to him as one of the best presenters on television. Well, at least he got that bit right.

However, having completed those important 'thank yous', his speech would go downhill as he resorted to a lot of pointless flannel in order to build up to his main point. The grand finale was to make sure that everyone was aware of how cheap *Gardeners' World* was to make, so cheap that it topped the BBC chart of programmes generating the highest number of viewers per pound spent on production.

Even though he knew it was coming, Dad was always incensed by this boast and therefore by the BBC. He spent many a long hour each year trying to persuade the people who held the programme's purse strings for more money, not for himself but to do more for the viewers' benefit. I have already mentioned his determination in the face of adversity; even though he was reminded each year of how much the BBC liked the fact that *Gardeners' World* was cheap to make, it did not stop him from asking in the faint hope that miracles sometimes do happen.

Fortunately Dad had spent most of his adult life gardening with little or no money, so making the best with what he had came naturally to him.

Money-saving projects were unquestionably the most popular features in the programme, but what else could he do on the budget he'd been given? However, he didn't dwell on the financial restrictions because, if nothing else, they put him on par with the average gardener who was watching. Dad conjured up ingenious and inventive designs so successfully that we never really understood the process from an initial idea to the successful end result.

Dad became so well known for this that it threatened to override everything else he wanted to do, but hidden deep in his psyche was another, less obvious trait: he was a bit of a technophobe. This was such a contrast to his horticultural and television life, where he was always on the lookout for the newest thing on the market. He was often the first to bring an innovation to the gardening public's attention (although sometimes he would dissect it first and come up with a similar product for a fraction of the price) but in his regular life he often looked with disdain at modern advances. He felt that many so-called modern advances were not better than tried-and-tested products and practices that had been around for decades – or even millennia. For example, he looked at the computer with great distrust compared to his loyal and trusted servant, his typewriter.

Writing books, as well as articles for gardening

magazines and the gardening section in national newspapers, was something he continued throughout his time on *Gardeners' World* but whilst everyone around him invested in a computer, he did not. He was adamant that his typewriter was just as good as this newfangled, modern contraption that need something called a 'floppy disc' inserted into it instead of paper.

He continued to send hard copies of his articles until the fateful day when the editor of a newspaper he was writing for told him that they would now only accept his copy on floppy disc. Dad's initial reaction was 'What's wrong with them?' – until the editor told him that was the only contributor who'd been sending in his articles on paper *for the last two years*! Everyone else had modernised.

It was as if Dad's life had just imploded. If this editor had told him to jump off the edge of the Niagara Falls to see if he could survive, he would have been more enthusiastic. He tried to fight the inevitable for as long as he could, but it was not that long at all; I think he felt an obligation to object and battle on even though he knew he would have to concede in the end.

He hung onto his old typewriter for the rest of his life, tucked away in its sturdy case and stuck in the corner of his office, because it was an old friend and something he hoped he could eventually go back to. He told me he kept it in case his newfangled machine broke down, as it inevitably would, but he did not fool me.

He was quite sad when he invested in a computer, not

because he was against spending the money but because he was suffering from the same feelings you have when your first car, the one that served you so well, has to be replaced. Although I still vividly remember my first car and talk about it affectionally, I have a blurrier memory of the ones that came after. This may be the reason why I also have my Dad's old typewriter in its case in the corner of *my* office!

The modern world was gathering pace and moving too fast for him; if he thought the computer was bad, there was worse to come: he had not yet encountered the mobile phone. These had started life as expensive executives' toys but rapidly dropped in price and became smaller. Soon they could be slipped into a pocket and became a 'must have' for billions of people around the world.

There were few people who felt no need for a phone that you could carry around with you wherever you went, but Dad was one of that exclusive group. As with the transition from typewriter to computer, he managed to avoid getting a mobile phone for way longer than he should have done, though the pressure was building. His wife, Lynda, was keen for him to have one so that she could get hold of him in an emergency when he was not at Barnsdale.

It was 1995 and this technology had crept into virtually everyone's life but Dad dug in his heels, adamant that he was happy with the phone that sat proudly on the hall table and was attached to the wall.

He had only just mastered pushing buttons instead of turning the central dial with his index finger, and he was not ready to move onto anything else.

This was not actually technophobia. Dad used all the excuses he'd employed in the typewriter-versus-computer standoff, but the real reason he resisted the mobile phone had nothing to do with technology: it was all about tranquillity.

He didn't need to take a phone with him because if someone called and needed to speak to him urgently while he was in his garden, Lynda would find him. The last thing he needed was people contacting him and disturbing his greatest pleasure, gardening.

In this day and age that seems an archaic view. Many people now seem to be welded to their phones; they go off at all times of the day and night and are immediately answered verbally or by text. Back in the mid-1990s, the mobile phone was nowhere near as important and Dad saw it as another unnecessary addition to our already overly technological lives.

The impact of a mobile phone on his gardening was not the only problem; his real concern was about the times he was driving. His car was his sanctuary, not a place he particularly enjoyed but the only one where he could think without being disturbed.

When he explained to me that this was his reason for flatly refusing to have a mobile phone, he said something that worried me about the quality of his driving. He explained that he did a lot of his thinking in his car; many of his ideas were born there because he had the time, solitude and head space to be mentally creative.

I understood and appreciated everything he said – but if he was doing that then how on earth was he also concentrating on his driving? But I decided not to question him, being fully aware that apart from his speeding offences there had been no other indiscretions.

He'd dug in his heels about a mobile phone so Lynda had to change tack. 'What about a pager?' she asked. Her idea was that in an emergency she could make him aware that he needed to phone her when he got the chance.

It turned out that to Dad a pager was also unnecessary technology. However, about a week after the idea had been mooted and dismissed, he had a phone call from someone on Channel 4's *Big Breakfast* production team. This early-morning programme was hosted by Gaby Roslin and Zoe Ball, and the production team wanted Dad to contribute to a short piece they were making on gardening.

Dad's agent, Steve Pink, phoned him with the proposal and Dad, who had no knowledge of the programme, had only one question: 'What type of programme is it?' He was a newspaper and coffee person first thing in the morning and never switched on the television.

Steve gave him an overview of the *Big Breakfast*, knowing that a more detailed description would only risk a negative response, but as soon as Dad realised that it was a young person's television show, he agreed to appear without even asking what was required of him.

He didn't follow youth culture so he had no idea how popular this programme was with its young adult audience, and it was not its popularity that was the deal breaker; Dad saw the opportunity to put gardening in front of a younger audience and break the myth that it was the preserve of old fuddy-duddies. He was definitely up for anything that might do that!

While he was talking excitedly to Steve, another question popped into his head – one he had not considered until then: would his appearance be live or recorded and shown at a later date?

Steve knew Dad could not shake off his dislike of live television, so he was happy to tell him that it would be recorded. The only fly in the ointment was that Dad thought they would want him for filming straight after the live show had finished, while everyone was available, which would mean setting off for London at some ungodly hour in the morning.

On the day, it turned out that filming was scheduled for after lunchtime so he didn't have to leave home while it was still dark. At 10am he said his goodbyes to Lynda before leaping into his Land Rover and setting off to the 'Old Smoke'. Having been born in the East End of London, Dad used this term with great affection.

He set off with Lynda's words ringing in his ears: 'Phone me when you get there so that I know you made it.' She watched his Land Rover turn right at the end of the drive and disappear before going back to finish her cup of coffee that was still sitting on the kitchen table.

No sooner had she walked through the door when the phone in the hall started to ring. She picked it up, curious as to who was phoning that early in the morning. It was Channel 4: apparently the camera they had used for the live programme (and that they were going to use to shoot Dad's gardening piece) had broken so they wanted to reschedule the filming for another day.

As Dad had been gone for less than five minutes, Lynda wanted to catch him and save him a long, pointless drive to London. I was in the potting shed on our Barnsdale Plants nursery, happily potting away, when the phone rang. Lynda rapidly described the situation and asked if I could catch up with him because he definitely wouldn't have got too far. Obviously she'd forgotten how Dad drove.

As usual I was the only person on the nursery but it was one of the two days in the week when we were not open to the public. I didn't need to be asked twice; I locked the nursery gate, leapt into my old banger and whizzed off towards the A1 south with a vague notion that I might catch Dad before he reached the motorway.

I was focused on my goal rather than the law or police, and I pushed my accelerator pedal to the floor of my blue Ford Escort estate. This was a classic car in that the mileage dial had almost gone full circle by the time I'd bought it and the bodywork was held together by narrow strands of rust; however, it was a workhorse which, given a good long straight piece of road, had once reached a magnificent 83mph! If I could achieve this feat again and Dad stuck to the speed limit, I had a chance of reeling him in.

I got to the A1 without seeing his Land Rover so I took the London turning and pulled onto the arterial road hoping that I would not reach the capital city. I had a good wind behind me and my foot was pressing so firmly on the accelerator that I feared it might go right through the floor of the car.

The speedometer gradually increased passed 60mph, then 70mph – and so did the vibrations in this old rust bucket. By the time the speedometer touched 80mph, the vibrations were so vigorous that I dare not attempt to achieve a new record of 84mph for fear of the car disintegrating. It felt like I was driving on the original North Road when it was cobbled!

Dad had told me that the days of him driving around 'foot to the floor' were long gone and that his driving had become much more sedate. He said that, when time allowed, he always took the more beautiful routes rather than the faster, more direct roads because it suited his new driving style. He had lied! I was now passing the Peterborough turning and there was still no sign of him.

I suddenly realised that I was leaning forward over the steering wheel, obviously trying to making myself more aerodynamic, a trick I'd learned as a sixteen-year-old while riding my moped, but somehow it didn't have the same effect in a car.

I was so determined to catch Dad that I didn't notice that the vibrations had increased to a level I'd not experienced before. When I realised what was happening, I looked at my speedometer. My 'knee-jerk' reaction was just that – I jerked my knee back to relieve the pressure on the accelerator because my speedometer needle was quivering around the 95mph mark!

I have no idea why I then checked my rear-view mirror to see if there was a police car behind me because it would have been far too late if there had been. Unlike Dad at my age, I was concerned to keep my driving licence clean.

Looking back, I realise that I'd been swept up in the panic of it all. By then I was approaching the Cambridge services and was resigned to Dad being too far ahead to catch, so I pulled in. If nothing else, I needed a coffee.

When I returned to my car, coffee in hand, I noticed that my driver's wing mirror was leaning away from the car; the vibrations had cracked the plastic housing! I needed to fix it before I set off home. Like all good nurserymen, I not only had my knife in my jeans' pocket but also some string. Once I'd tied the damaged wing mirror back onto its moorings, I set off at a much more sedate (and legal) pace back to Barnsdale.

Later that evening Dad returned home and to say that he was not in a jolly mood would have been a massive understatement – you could still see the steam coming out of his ears! In an attempt to lighten the atmosphere, and for reasons known only to herself, Lynda decided to mention that if he'd had a phone or pager she could have contacted him before he'd even got to the end of the road to stop him travelling all that way for nothing. That took the wind out of his sails because he knew that she was right, but he was a stubborn old bugger and still flatly refused to get either.

To add insult to injury, the Channel 4 recording was never rescheduled.

◻◻◻

Dad was such a natural at television presenting that the fear he had of live television seemed disproportionate. Virtually everything he filmed for *Gardeners' World* was perfect on the first take; he rarely needed a second go so that was akin to doing it live. I suppose the big difference was that he knew that if he messed up he could stop and go again, a luxury not afforded with live television where the pressure was on him to get it right first time, every time. The fear of the unexpected or everything going pear-shaped meant he worried about ending up looking like an idiot in front of millions of viewers.

When pushed – and only when pushed very, very hard – he would concede to a live appearance. A perfect example of this was his appearance on *Comic Relief*.

It was early 1993, and those who make the decisions at the BBC thought *Gardeners' World* should do the honourable thing and take part in the programme. The powers-that-be liked charity events, so the team was already committed and, as Dad was its lead presenter, it was expected that he would be involved. In those days it was as big a charitable event as it is now and, unexpectedly, he seemed keen to do his bit.

Dad was a charity-event veteran, having appeared on *Children in Need* in a combined effort with Lionel Blair – although Lionel was definitely the main star of the piece. Dad was more than happy with this set-up, although Lionel did hug him more often than he was comfortable with. The most important part of his charity appearance was that it was pre-recorded at Barnsdale and he agreed to *Comic Relief* thinking this would be the same.

The involvement of *Gardeners' World* was the gardening-related competition they would run on the programme for several weeks before the main charity evening. It was not until Dad was fully committed to the project that he found out that he wouldn't be picking the winners from the safety of his home at Barnsdale in a pre-recorded segment – he would be doing it live!

The *Comic Relief* production team were very good. They decided to ask him to push a wheelbarrow full of numbered red noses onto the set and join a well-known comedian in front of the cameras to pick the winners. That was all they told him, so that was all he knew; at that point they said they didn't know which comedian it would be, but Dad would be briefed when he arrived at the BBC studios.

He didn't feel completely at ease having to do this live but was comforted by the thought that he had very little to do. His index fingers and thumbs were dextrous enough for him to pick out the winning noses quickly and the whole thing would take less than two minutes; what could possibly go wrong?

Having arrived at the BBC, he spent a comfortable hour and a half in the Green Room helping himself to food and coffee before eventually being called. He slid on the wellies he'd been asked to bring along and pulled on the *Comic Relief* T-shirt he'd been asked to wear, then prepared to show the millions watching who weren't *Gardeners' World* viewers how professionally he could push a wheelbarrow.

The barrow was full to the brim with plant pots containing red noses. The only briefing Dad got was that he needed to push it on, be greeted by the presenter, pick out five noses and hand them to the presenter. Once this simple task was completed, he could turn and retreat off stage.

He was ushered from the Green Room to the side of the set. Readying himself for his cue, he waited for the word; when it came, he assumed a happy, smiling face and put his best wellied foot forward. He had only had to walk three paces before he was in shot and could see who he was walking towards.

Immediately Dad's healthy complexion started to pale. Now Dad liked the comedian Ruby Wax a lot; he found her brand of comedy right up his street mainly because she was unpredictable and a bit of a loose cannon, which made her live appearances even funnier.

As he stepped onto the set that thought hit him like a runaway train – not that he found her very funny but that she was unpredictable. He tentatively approached the beaming Ruby Wax who was obviously pleased to see him despite his face now resembling that of a fashionable, white-faced Elizabethan. I'm sure the corners of his mouth started to quiver at that point but her smile was so wide it made her teeth glisten under the studio lights. He looked tentative and frightened as she opened her arms in a welcoming gesture but he couldn't hug her as both his hands were firmly attached to the handles of his wheelbarrow.

I watched the situation unfold from the comfort of my living room at home under no doubt that this was probably one of the most uncomfortable moments he had ever encountered.

He was terrified as to what would come out of her mouth so he was both surprised and relieved when her opening line was, 'Hello, Geoff. So nice to see you.'

You could see the relief in his eyes as he replied, 'Thanks very much, it's lovely to be here.'

Ruby turned to the camera to give a quick run-through of the basics of the *Gardeners' World / Comic Relief* competition before turning to Dad and asking him to select the first winner.

He was starting to settle down and relax; this was going well. Then, just as he bent down to pick the first red nose from the wheelbarrow, Ruby floored him with a right hook that he never saw coming.

'Ooh, I do like a man with fertile fingers!' she announced loudly.

The only time I'd seen the blood drain from Dad's face so quickly was the day I had appeared at home unexpectedly having punched my teacher and run away from primary school.

The bright studio lights that were lighting up Ruby's beaming smile enhanced Dad's ghost-like face. It was rare that he was lost for words but this was definitely one of those moments. It was as if he'd been floored by Mohamed Ali and he was definitely 'out for the count'.

All he could think of was to pick the winners and get off the set as quickly as possible, so his fertile fingers worked as fast as they could to select the remaining winners' noses. He passed the last one to Ruby, she thanked him and he literally ran off the stage, pushing his wheelbarrow as fast as his wobbly legs would carry him. Afterwards he still loved to watch Ruby Wax – but he vowed never to do live television again.

Some people take to live television and some don't. Dad was definitely in the 'don't' camp, although I am 100% certain that if Ruby Wax's comment had been made off screen he would have shot back an equally hilarious remark without even thinking.

At the end of the day there was no real harm done, apart from Dad being mentally scarred by the trauma he had just endured. It could have been a lot worse; he came away virtually unscathed and had done his bit for charity, so everyone was a winner.

As he retreated back into the safe world of pre-recorded television, he discovered other benefits to working for the BBC. It turned out that the Corporation pay an extra appearance fee if the programme you are featured in is repeated. This was not something the main presenter of *Gardeners' World* had needed to worry about because each programme was specific to the time of year it was broadcast. Even if the same tasks were carried out the following year, all producer/directors liked to film them in a different way. From time to time the BBC is vilified in the press for repeating comedy and drama programmes too frequently, but due to their time-specific nature *Gardeners' World* programmes were not suitable for repeating.

Dad started each morning with breakfast and a morning cuppa at the kitchen table, and usually he finished off reading the previous day's newspaper knowing that he would soon have the post to go through. His postman was a bit of an early bird so the mail landed on his doormat mid-breakfast. This particular morning was no different.

He had just finished the unread bits of his newspaper when a bunch of letters hit the floor with a thud. He put down his mug of coffee and hauled himself from his chair to see what delights the postman had brought. He shuffled through them as he always did, putting letters that he thought contained payments to the front and any that looked like bills to the back of the pile. Unknowns were sandwiched in the middle.

He knew that he had a gift (or at least he had convinced himself that he had a gift); some years earlier he had told me that he could smell the money inside envelopes before he opened them. It was a skill he had apparently honed over many years and he was now at the peak of his powers. He told me this in a confident tone; when his sons were young and naïve he had no problem in convincing us of his abilities and we had believed a lot of utter rubbish over the years. However, there comes a time when parents should accept that children now recognise that both Father Christmas and the Tooth Fairy were not real, but occasionally you get a parent who just won't let go of a great idea, irrespective of their child's age. Dad was definitely one of those. He loved telling us his tall tales and flatly refused to stop.

Everyone knew that his bills usually arrived in brown envelopes with the window at the front showing what they were. Cheques, on the other hand, were enclosed in a white envelope of better quality and often with the company name printed on the reverse. Even so, there seemed to be no option but to play along with his 'smelling money' ruse just to keep an old and delusional man happy!

This was not turning out to be a good day; he deduced that there were far more bills than cheques. As always, he began by opening the envelopes he was fairly sure contained remuneration and left the bills and those he was unsure about until later. He felt that his positive mindset after a long, enjoyable period in his garden would help cushion the blow he would encounter from the pile of bills on his return to the kitchen table.

There were only two envelopes that smelled as if they contained payment. Just to play it safe, he started with the one stamped with the BBC return address on the back. He was 100% certain that this contained a cheque, not just because he had a paranormal gift but also because of the BBC element.

Even so, he was somewhat confused because all his BBC work was paid via his agent and put straight into his bank account. The Corporation never sent payments directly to him, so was it possible that his paranormal powers had thrown him a curve ball? Was it in fact a bill or – even worse – a P45?

He dismissed these negative thoughts in favour of a more shocking one that popped into his head: was this a letter telling him that the BBC had given him a pay rise? That idea almost took his breath away until he quickly realised that would never happen. Oh no! He was back onto the P45!

He tentatively slid his index finger under the corner of the flap, ran it across the length of the envelope and only looked at the contents with one eye in order to soften the blow. When he realised it contained *both* a letter and a cheque, he opened his other eye just to make sure. How odd: the letter was from the BBC, but what was it and why was there a cheque?

Whatever amount it was for would not give him the answer, so he put it down and went to the letter. There were no pleasantries; it was short and to the point with three lines of typing to tell him that he'd received this payment for his appearance on BBC1's *Eastenders*. How strange: he had never watched an episode of *Eastenders*, let alone appeared in one!

He put down the letter and picked up the cheque in the vain hope that it might lead him to the answer, but it only left him even more perplexed. His first thought was that the BBC had sent it in error and maybe, just maybe, if he dashed straight to the bank and deposited it they wouldn't realise what they had done. Having decided that, in his opinion, he had been underpaid for years it could be deemed a bonus for the things he had given for free to the BBC.

He eagerly glanced at the amount then scrunched up his eyes in case that made a difference. He opened them properly and looked again: surely they had missed at least one or, if they were feeling generous, two noughts off the total?

No, he had read it correctly the first time: the staggering amount they had sent him was for £3!

Three pounds – what the hell was that for? He was certainly paid more than that for each *Gardeners' World* appearance – not a lot more, but certainly double figures. He put the cheque on the table hoping that something would come to him to solve this mystery but after fifteen minutes he was still none the wiser.

He decided to do the honourable thing and disappear into his garden where he could let his thought processes roam free.

Unfortunately this time, his tried-and-tested method failed and he returned to the kitchen table and the troublesome cheque none the wiser. Depressingly, the only thing he had come up with was that maybe the BBC had reduced his paltry presenter's fee to single figures. There was nothing for it, he would have to sacrifice the possibility of an unexpected bonus and phone the BBC to find out what was going on.

Having phoned the main switchboard, he was eventually put through to a lady in the accounts department who, after checking, told Dad that the cheque was payment of a repeat fee, though she didn't know any more than that. It had been issued by the BBC accounts department but she didn't know why it was for an appearance on *Eastenders*.

Dad had a flash of the blindingly obvious. John Kenyon knew everyone at the BBC, or it certainly seemed that way to Dad, and he could certainly track down the answer.

Dad had already experienced John's encyclopaedic knowledge of the BBC staff, and it was not long before he had the answer; apparently Dad had appeared on *Eastenders* in a scene taking place in the Fowler household when a *Gardeners' World* programme had been playing on their television in the background! It was something that had been filmed at Barnsdale with

Dad presenting.

John was proud to have solved Dad's mystery though the explanation meant nothing to Dad because he had no idea who the Fowler family were and why he should be receiving a repeat fee. It turned out that even if you are heard on the radio in another television programme or seen on television in the background of a drama scene, it is BBC policy that you receive a repeat fee. The fee is modified to represent the amount of television time taken up by this 'repeat'.

Dad was gobsmacked, not at the policy even though he thought that this attention to detail was praiseworthy, but at the staggering cost of issuing such a meagre cheque. He was pretty sure that it cost the BBC at least ten times more than the cheque was worth for the whole process to be carried out.

At least the cheque's value saved a dash to Barclays because he never banked it, electing to display it proudly on his oddities' cork board in the downstairs toilet as one of the strangest things he had ever been sent.

Chapter Seven

Dad was very proud of living in Rutland and would extol the beautiful countryside, chocolate-box villages and rural nature, as well as the peace and quiet of the England's smallest county. He often told friends and colleagues that Rutland was so safe that he left his front door and Land Rover unlocked at night and even, on occasion, left the car keys in the ignition. In hindsight this probably was not the best idea, because any passing opportunist could steal his car or break into his house. Inevitably, his determination to tell all and sundry about the safety of Rutland ended up having far-reaching effects.

By the 1990s, the filming of *Gardeners' World* had changed enormously, particularly with the dramatic drop in the number of crew members needed at Barnsdale. The outside broadcast lorries were no longer used so all editing was done back at base in Birmingham, and the number of cameramen had dropped from three to one. Most of this small crew drove from Birmingham to Barnsdale in a BBC pool car, which had to be signed in and out as these cars were not owned by the BBC but leased from a separate company so a paper trail had to be created. This was important because it covered the BBC if anything happened to one of the cars.

In the week before a very unfortunate event occurred, and during a break in filming, Dad had been eulogising the lack of criminality in rural Rutland to the crew, again using the story about his unlocked car. One of the crew listening intensely to his glorification of crime-free Rutland was an impressionable, naïve young BBC runner.

For those not in the know about the role of a runner, it has nothing to do with athletics although they do spend a lot of their time dashing from one place to the next. The runner is a general assistant who usually works under the direction of the producer / director. For *Gardeners' World*, this meant making sure all the equipment was in place and ready for filming, the camera and sound person had what they needed, timing each piece that was shot, fetching the tea and coffee and anything else required to ensure the smooth running of the event.

This particular young woman was selected for filming at Barnsdale the following week, too. As she had done previously, she ordered, signed for and collected her pool car before tootling over to Barnsdale. Being young and keen to do well, she set off in plenty of time and arrived a good forty minutes earlier than anyone else.

Rather than disturb Dad before the agreed arrival time, she thought she'd take the chance to have a good look around his garden. She'd only been to Barnsdale once before, so the only parts she'd seen were those she'd passed while rushing from one task to another. With Dad's words still fresh in her mind, she left her keys in the car and disappeared into the garden.

The most important part of this story is to understand that neither Dad nor the crew parked their cars on the roadside or in view of the road. Dad's house and garden were hidden behind a strip of beech trees; cars were only visible when someone turned into his driveway and arrived in front of the house, which is why he felt so confident about leaving his car unlocked all the time.

The rest of the crew arrived, parked, locked their cars and set off for a cup of tea before filming started. Nobody noticed that the car that had already arrived was unlocked with the key dangling in the ignition.

It was a beautiful day and the morning's filming went without a hitch, so they decided to take lunch early; if the afternoon's filming went just as well, they'd finish early too. The runner went to collect the packed lunch she'd left in her car – but as she rounded the side of the house the car was no longer parked where she had left it…

She burst through the back door of the house screaming hysterically, 'My car's gone! My car's gone!' before crumpling into a sobbing heap on a kitchen chair.

Being the sensible one, the only thing Dad could think to ask was, '*Where* has your car gone?'

'It's been stolen!' she screamed.

Dad and the producer followed her outside and she pointed at the empty spot where the pool car should have been. All Dad could think to say was, 'Oh.'

By this point the tears were flowing as she started to worry about how she was going to explain to her boss that the car had been stolen. When he found out that she'd parked it and left it unlocked with the keys in the ignition, he would not be pleased. Worse than that, it could be the end of her fledgling BBC career.

The police were called. After taking the details and lots of tutting about the keys in the ignition, they offered a glimmer of hope that these vehicles usually turn up abandoned somewhere fairly close by.

A couple of days later, Dad discovered what had actually happened to the car and precisely how and when it was stolen. At the time there was an open prison about two miles away and a prisoner had decided that he couldn't endure the remaining three months of his custodial sentence. An opportunity had arisen for him to abscond and he had decided that cross country was his best route.

It happened to be the day filming was taking place at Barnsdale when he set off across the fields. He soon found himself trotting through the field gate that led to the front of Dad's house.

One of the many crimes that had led to him being incarcerated was car theft and now he was facing a row of unattended cars. Being proficient in hot-wiring, his first thought was to try the doors of each vehicle in case he got lucky. To his amazement, the first car he tried was unlocked! His amazement turned to ecstasy when he saw that there was a key already in the ignition. It was as if someone had left his getaway car primed and ready for him so, after thanking the god of getaway drivers, he leapt in and sped off.

The thing was that during Dad's espousing of the quietness of the county, the lack of criminality, etc, etc, he'd not once mentioned escaping prisoners. Admittedly the prison was low category so the prisoners sent there were being prepared for release and deemed not dangerous to the public, and this was very much the situation in this case.

The problem was that Dad was not blessed with a flash of inspiration as to how this young lady would reply when her boss asked her the inevitable question. He only hoped that she would not say, 'I did it because Geoff told me to.'

There was a glimmer of light in this whole depressing incident because she went home with the cameraman who lived within striking distance of her house. The following day she faced her boss and explained in great detail exactly what had happened to the car, up to the point where she'd left it parked in front of Dad's house.

Her boss listened to the explanation and started to explain that the insurance company would probably not pay out for a car that was left unlocked with the keys in the ignition. He stopped, not wanting to add that this combination made it ripe for stealing, so this left a stony silence. At just the right moment, the phone rang. It was a Rutland police officer who said that the pool car had been found twenty miles away in perfect condition, with the keys still in the ignition, and would he like to come and pick it up?

'No I would not,' was his reply. 'But I know somebody who would love to!'

This young woman at the start of her television career was saved from any recrimination and cost, although she was left in no doubt that this sort of thing was never to happen again. Dad also learned from this episode and from then on always removed the keys from the ignition when he arrived home – even though he usually failed to lock the car or the front door of the house because that would have been a step too far. This had been a once-in-a-lifetime experience, and he was determined that nobody would spoil his idyllic lifestyle – even after having his own Land Rover stolen!

He and Lynda had booked a well-deserved winter holiday to Goa on the west coast of India. Dad had never been one for package holidays; he preferring to organise trips himself. This time, unlike the Cornwall camping holidays we experienced as children, he decided to arrange their accommodation before leaving, which was a massive organisational step forward from his usual practice of arriving and hoping to find something.

He took the expert opinion of a travel agent and the trip was meticulously planned well before they stepped onto the plane. Another first was that, rather than trouble anyone to take them to and pick them up from the airport, they would park the Land Rover in the Heathrow Airport secure car park. This was apparently as secure as they got and it meant that, with the return flight arriving at around midday and Dad invariably able to grab some sleep on the flight back, the car would be waiting for them. The couple of hours drive home would be no problem at all.

After a last-minute check that their passports were stored in Lynda's bag, off they set. At the secure car park, all they needed to do was input their registration details into a machine, retrieve the printed ticket and park the car.

They had a fabulous two weeks in and around Goa, although half way through the second week Dad started to miss his garden and was itching to get back to it. As the plane landed at Heathrow, he had already worked out their approximate time of arrival at Barnsdale; he'd be able to squeeze in at least an hour of gardening before the winter light beat him and he could no longer see. That put him in a good mood – although that was about to change as he left the terminal building and hit the fresh, cold, British air.

Having carefully selected the airport luggage trolley so that they got one that didn't have a mind of its own, they set off towards the car park – only to find that the trolley did have a mind of its own and seemed determined to go in a different direction. This tested

Dad's resolve but he remained focused on getting his hands back into Barnsdale soil.

As they approached the secure car parking area, he reached inside his jacket pocket to retrieve the parking ticket. It was a bit premature because the ticket was only required when they drove out, but he wanted to ensure a smooth passage. He'd also had the foresight to make a mental note of where the car was parked; this made it very easy to find – or more precisely to find the empty parking bay where the Land Rover should have been.

His first thought was that he had mis-remembered the parking spot, so he left the trolley with Lynda and wandered up and down the rows of cars. No, it was definitely nowhere to be seen. Now what were they supposed to do? He had never had a car stolen before, so wasn't quite sure of the procedure. Should he phone 999 because it was sort of an emergency, though it was not a life-threatening situation?

Having considered his options he decided to speak to the man in the exit booth and show him his ticket. This jolly man told him that he needed to bring his car in order to leave the car park, to which Dad replied that he would if the car was still where he'd left it. The jolly parking-booth man's face dropped and he picked up his telephone to summon his supervisor to deal with the matter. This was apparently way above his pay grade.

Once the supervisor had established that the Land Rover was definitely no longer there, he told Dad and Lynda that he had to call the police as it had definitely been stolen. Fortunately, being London, the police arrived in minutes and started taking details whilst also informing Dad that his beloved car had most likely been stolen to order and was probably already on its way to the Middle East. Apparently this was a known route for these vehicles at the time because they were in great demand.

Dad was confused; surely the residents of the oil-rich nations could afford to buy new Land Rovers? And how on earth could a criminal steal a vehicle from a secure car park? This was the question he posed to the police officer but the reply he got was certainly not the one he was expecting.

At the time the car park worked on a system that they deemed was as secure as they could get. When travellers arrived, they put their car registration details into a machine that dispensed a printed ticket with those details on it. If you took the ticket on holiday with you, your car was secure because you were the only person with that ticket. On your return, you presented it to the person in the booth, they checked the registration number on the ticket was the same as that of the car and let you out.

Dad was fully aware of this process but the policeman reiterated it anyway and continued with the important information that Dad did *not* know. Criminals stole a car from the secure car park by driving in, getting their ticket then driving around until they identified a car they wanted to steal. They noted its registration plate number and left the car park, having paid a small fee for their short stay. They returned the next day, usually in an old banger, and put the registration number of the car they wanted to steal into the machine – not the one they'd driven in with. After breaking into the car they wanted, they drove it to the kiosk where its plate and ticket were checked, and then off they went.

Dad was utterly gobsmacked at how easy it was to steal a car from a car park advertised as 'safe and secure'.

The policeman was very understanding; Dad's was not the first car to go missing from the car park and definitely wouldn't be the last while this system was in place.

Dad was about to tell him that this sort of thing would never happen in Rutland but fortunately he remembered the 'pool car episode'. No matter how sympathetic the policeman was, this was not going to get them home and, just to rub extra salt into his wound, certainly not home in time for him to get into his garden before it got dark!

They filled in the paperwork for both the policeman and the car park supervisor and phoned for a taxi. Dad was positive that the company that ran the car park (or his own insurance company) would reimburse him. The flight had been a long one and he and Lynda just wanted to get home.

The following day they woke very early, still on Goa time, but managed to go back to sleep until mid-morning. Dad knew that the first thing he must was phone his insurance company. He passed on the crime number the policeman had given him to the insurance person, then answered the same questions he'd gone through the previous day with both the police and car-park supervisor.

Never having been in this situation before, he was pleasantly surprised when they offered him a courtesy car and told him that the claim was likely to take a few weeks to process. I have no idea what he had said on the phone, but within only two weeks the cheque popped though the letterbox and Dad rushed down to the bank before setting off to invest in a brand-new Land Rover.

This happened a couple of years before he passed away. Once he'd received his cheque from the insurance company he thought nothing more about his stolen car – apart from reciting this experience every time the opportunity arose.

When he died, Lynda sold his two-year-old Land Rover; then, about eighteen months later, I received a phone call out of the blue from a Metropolitan police detective inspector who wanted to speak to Mr Hamilton.

Having two brothers, I asked which one he wanted to speak to. When he said, 'Geoff Hamilton,' this was definitely the Hamilton I was not expecting. The first thing that popped into my head was a quip about a Ouija board but my generation was well aware that the Metropolitan Police did not mess around, so I decided on a serious answer.

I explained what had happened to Dad and asked why the inspector wanted to speak to him. The answer was not at all what I expected. Essex police had pulled over a Land Rover because, according to their database, its plates did not match the vehicle they were on. The chap driving it was a prolific petty criminal who was well known to them and it turned out that Dad's Land Rover had never made it to the Middle East – it had only got as far as Middle Essex. Although the police finally found it, it was too late for Dad; the car was sent to the insurance company because they'd become its proud owners as soon as he'd received his payout cheque.

I have no idea why, but our family seems to attract problems involving the constabulary without ever having committed a crime and certainly never being arrested. A classic example of this was the strange experience I had when living in digs and working in Norfolk.

One night I was coming back from yet another classic Spear of Destiny concert at the Hammersmith Palais in London. It was 1.30am and I was feeling very tired but thankful that I was almost home; I had just turned onto a seven-mile stretch of straight road that meant I was only ten miles from my bed.

I had hurtled about half the length of this road when I saw a single beam of light in the distance hovering about a metre above the ground. Over the next half mile or so, worried that I was so tired I'd started to hallucinate and to improve my vision to see what was happening ahead, I rubbed my eyes a few times. Unfortunately that had no positive effect.

I slowed a bit and partially closed my eyelids to try and identify this mysterious light, but that only made it move slowly from side to side. I wondered whether I was seeing a UFO; after all, I was in the wilds of Norfolk and these things do tend to happen in those sorts of places. However, after what seemed an age, my headlights revealed a very human figure emerging out of the pitch-black night in front of me.

I rapidly identified it as a policeman dressed in full (and very dark) uniform with no hi-vis. He was standing on my side of the road holding a torch.

I rubbed my eyes again, just to make sure this was really happening and not a figment of my tired imagination, but he was still there.

As he approached the driver's side of the car, I wound down my window. He leaned in and asked where I'd been, bearing in mind how late it was. I had never been stopped by the police before and felt somewhat aggrieved to be stopped on this road at this time of night just so that he could find out where I'd been; that was the sort of question I would have expected from a worried father, not a local bobby.

I subdued my irritation but, on the spur of the moment, decided to tell him that it was none of his business! Looking back, I have no idea why I suddenly became so belligerent but I was absolutely certain of one thing: he would have no idea who Spear of Destiny were, so answering his question was pointless. He took a long, hard look at me then waved me on my way.

As I continued to my digs, the thing playing on my mind was why a policeman had been standing four miles down a long, quiet country road at 1.30am. If he was expecting to catch a drink driver or two, it must have been a hell of a 'lock-in' at the local pubs for them to be falling out of the door at that time. I really don't know if he spoke to anyone else that evening, so all these years later I still have no answer to my question.

That police encounter continues to be one of the oddest occurrences in my life, though it was eventually beaten into second place by another. That was related to the unfortunate disappearance of Derek and Eileen Severs, who had been reported missing from their home in the village of Hambleton about four miles away from Barnsdale.

Their disappearance was reported on Thursday 18th November 1993 but my involvement in this episode began on the morning of Sunday 21st November. I was, as I had been on every Sunday morning for the previous three years, pottering about on the nursery and waiting for my first customer; I'd arrived at 8.30am and was open from 10am. I remember it wasn't particularly cold for that time of year so I was expecting a reasonably busy day because it was also the perfect time of year for planting.

I had slightly later opening and earlier closing times

in the winter months. Sundays always seemed to start more slowly than the other six days of the week, but this particular one was incredibly quiet and by lunchtime I hadn't seen a single customer.

I was starting to worry about my daily revenue but, being an optimist, I ate my lunch as quickly as I could in readiness for that first customer to appear; I certainly did not want to greet someone with my mouth stuffed full of cheese-and-pickle sandwich. Unfortunately this rapid lunch had no effect on the customer flow and in the afternoon we had as many customers as in the morning: none.

In the three years since the nursery had opened, I'd never had a weekend day with such good weather and not a single customer. There had been days when it was tipping down with rain, incredibly cold or the country completely covered with snow when nobody had visited, but that was to be expected. I was desolate.

I was so upset at this missed income-making opportunity that I locked up and was in my car just before my 4pm closing time, ready to head off to see Dad and give him my daily report. As I turned left out of the nursery drive and headed the hundred metres along The Avenue to Dad's house, I saw a row of traffic cones across the road and a traffic sign beyond them. Scooting round the barrier by mounting the grass verge, I saw a police sign that said 'Road Closed', which frustrated me because it could have contributed to my nil-income day.

I was curious as to whether there was another road closed sign at the other end and, if there was, how long the road had been closed for. Although it was too late to rescue my trading day, I decided to find out.

I drove down country roads and along the main road and found exactly the same situation at the opposite end of The Avenue and my frustration grew. I'd been waiting in the nursery all day for customers who couldn't get to me because the road was closed at both ends – and whoever had cordoned it off the road had left me marooned in the middle!

I needed to find out how long the signs had been there for. As there were no police and nobody to ask what was going on, I decided to return to Barnsdale and moan about my predicament to Dad. He was equally gobsmacked, not only because nobody had told me about the road closure, but also because he didn't know what was going on. He was now as curious as I was.

Dad's calculating brain kicked in and he decided that the only way to find the answer was to phone the police. He had no plan of action; I think he was relying on the Hamilton quick wit and charm to get the information we both wanted.

He phoned Oakham police station and explained about the road: could they tell him why it had been closed? This copper would only say that he was not in a position to add anything to what Dad had already told him.

Even though he *was* sitting down, Dad certainly

was not going to take that type of answer sitting down! The Hamilton wit and charm were not the answer in this particular situation so he went all out instead, explaining to the policeman that he lived on that road so it was imperative that he knew what was going on. He then said something that surprised even me; he had obviously persuaded himself this was his only shot at finding out so he asked, 'Has the road been closed because of an IRA bomb?'

He didn't wait for an answer but pressed ahead, pointing out that he had the right to know for his and his family's safety. I was amazed that he was bringing the IRA into the equation since they had long-since stopped bombing mainland Britain, but Dad seemed proud of his quick thinking.

Needless to say, he got no joy from the policeman and he had nowhere else to go. Instead he had to be satisfied with the reply: 'I can tell you that it has nothing to do with the IRA.' That was the best he would get, so Dad signed off with a 'thank you very much'.

That was never going to be the end of it; once Dad got the bit between his teeth there was no letting go until he got exactly what he wanted. He vowed to try again in the morning when there would be a different, and perhaps more amenable, police employee at the other end of the line.

He only remembered to phone around lunchtime. Even with a gentler approach, he only got as far as he had done the previous day. This left us with no option but to wait for the news to be revealed when our local newspaper, *The Rutland Times*, went on sale.

On Wednesday afternoon Dad gave me the money – a rare enough event – and asked me to pick up a copy of the paper on my way to work the following morning. Even though Roger Severs had not yet been arrested in connection with the disappearance of his parents (which happened two days later), the front page of the newspaper had all the information we needed to satisfy our curiosity.

It emerged that Severs was the prime suspect in the disappearance and probable murder of his parents. The police were working on the assumption that he had buried their bodies locally because there was evidence that his father's car had recently been driven through woodland. Because of the beech twigs embedded in mud on the car tyres, the police suspected that his parents may have been buried in part of The Avenue and the only way to find out was to carry out a fingertip search through the woods either side of the road. The road was closed while this was carried out. Many police were involved, but it was still a painstaking, arduous and lengthy process that took all day.

My problem was the enthusiasm with which I had woken up that particular Sunday morning. By arriving at work an hour earlier than I usually did, the road was as it should have been – open. It was Sunday, so I'd turned the sign on the verge to 'open' at 10am and didn't notice the road being coned off and closed as I went back into work. I assume that when the policeman drove down the road to close off the end near Dad's house, they passed my 'Nursery Open' sign and chose to ignore it, preferring to leave me marooned for the day and wondering why nobody wanted to buy my plants.

Once it was determined that our lives were not under threat by the IRA, Dad realised how funny the situation was and particularly how hilarious it was that I'd spent all day waiting for cars to turn in from a sealed-off road. Although he had many a laugh at my expense, I found it much stranger that he thought the IRA would want to place a bomb where the impact of it exploding would be only to damage a few trees. I never did get round to asking for a full explanation.

On 1st December 1993 our curiosity was satisfied. The police discovered the bodies of Derek and Eileen Severs buried in woodland close to Rutland Water, not too far from their home. Roger Severs had already been charged with their murder and on the 6th of December 1994 he was convicted and received two life sentences.

Odd as that occurrence was, it just one in a reasonably long run of oddness that I encountered driven by my association with Dad. Some time before being marooned with no customers, and before I came back to work with Dad on a full-time basis, I was on my way to the Noel Arms in Whitwell when I happened on a French gendarme directing traffic on a British road. Funnily enough, this came as no surprise; it was a result of a seed sown on a rather inebriated night in the Noel

Arms in early 1980.

Several regulars had gathered in the pub, Dad included. They discussed a lot of current topics before Malcolm brought up the subject of how posh the town of Stamford was; he got the impression that our residents were almost sneered at every time that they entered it for not being from Stamford. (I think this may have been a combination of Malcolm having visited the town that day and the beer talking.)

For those of you who have never visited, Stamford is a town in south Lincolnshire with its western edge only one hundred metres from the Rutland border. It seems that the conversation had been instigated by Brian's return to the bar from what the pub regulars called 'the pissoir', the French term for a urinal.

After Malcolm's comment, the conversation veered wildly onto his distorted view of Stamford, his opinion based solely on the fact that it was twinned with a town in France that had the posh-sounding name of St-Paul-de-Vence. Since all the members of the group had by now drunk one too many Ruddles ales, they decided that the best thing to do was to get one over on Stamford and show them that Whitwell could be just as posh – or even posher!

With their brains now somewhat foggy and incapable of deep thought, the consensus was to find an even posher town in France to twin with. The problem was that none of them had actually been to St-Paul-de-Vence, so they had no idea how posh it actually was.

None of them had been further than Brittany except for Dad, who had visited Paris a couple of times, so coming up with a posher town for Whitwell to twin with would have been unlikely when they were all sober – and completely impossible in their current state.

That didn't stop them from trying. Having been fuelled by another drink or two, the only idea generated was that if they were planning to outdo Stamford, they should twin Whitwell with Paris! That would show the Stamfordians, and it would elevate Whitwell into top echelons of poshness. But how to go about it?

It is amazing how excitement can build over a ridiculous idea when fuelled by a Ruddles or two – or three or four. They were unanimous in their agreement that the first step should be to send a letter to the mayor of Paris the following day and, as it was Malcolm who had instigated the whole affair, he was tasked with the job.

It took slightly more than a day to complete, primarily due to the after-effects of the night before, but a letter was sent to Jacques Chirac, the incumbent mayor of Paris, asking if the city would like to be twinned with mighty Whitwell in Rutland, England. The regulars of the Noel Arms deemed this request very reasonable and one that the mayor would be foolish to turn down.

Having researched the two towns, it turns out that Stamford and St-Paul-de-Vence are well matched in their size and population, whereas Paris is a city with a population of around 8.5 million and Whitwell is a village with a steady population of just under fifty; not such a good match.

Having not received a reply after several weeks, they wrote to Monsieur Chirac again. This time they said that if they didn't receive a reply within a month of the date of the letter, Whitwell would assume that the mayor agreed with the twinning. This sparked the Parisian mayor into action and a reply was received within the time limit, though it wasn't what the self-styled Whitwell Twinning Committee had been expecting or had hoped for. The letter said very politely that unfortunately Paris was already twinned with Rome and that was the only city, town or village that they would be twinning with.

The committee members were certainly not going to take this sitting down – or more likely leaning against the bar – so they decided to plough on.

They immediately set in motion plans for a ceremony to mark the momentous union between Paris and mighty Whitwell. There was only one place suitable for such an important event and that was the only place in Whitwell with a French pissoir: the Noel Arms, of course. The date was set, a marquee was ordered, and all that was left to be done was to let the wider world know about it.

That meant contacting our two local newspapers, which would undoubtedly run a story. This publicity had a dual purpose: firstly, it was clear that there were not enough friends and family of the conspirators to make the event as momentous as it should be, so the wider public needed to be alerted; secondly, it was the best way to inform Stamford that Whitwell would soon be much posher than them, with a far superior twinning partner.

The plans were in place, friends and family had been alerted, so all that was left to do was to invite local dignitaries such as the Lord Lieutenant of Rutland, the leader of Rutland County Council, the High Sheriff of Rutland and, of course, Monsieur Jacques Chirac. Bearing in mind that Paris had no intention of twinning with Whitwell, that last invitation was more in hope than in expectation, but the committee felt it was only right and proper to issue it.

In case Jacques decided not to attend, Plan B was put in place. Authenticity was essential, and the only authentic French person they knew was a local French teacher who was primed and ready to go as the stand-in for the Mayor of Paris, beret at the ready!

Being his efficient self, Dad issued my party invite in a phone conversation a week before the ceremony but, as I found out later, the problem with a verbal invitation from Dad was that he failed to give me all the information. In fact, he failed to give me virtually any information.

He was so keen to make sure I'd come to the party at the Noel Arms that he failed to mention of the fact that it was a celebration of the twinning of Whitwell and Paris; more importantly, he didn't mention that it would be a Français fancy-dress party!

When the day of the party arrived, I had to travel

straight from my job on a glasshouse nursery in Hertfordshire. That meant I wouldn't arrive until the party was in full swing, so I decided to meet Dad at the pub.

As I drove into the village about two hours after the party had officially started, I noticed something unusual: close to the entrance of the pub car park a man was standing in the middle of the road. Having been to France many times and been driven through Paris, I was familiar with the sight of the back of a gendarme in full uniform directing traffic. The problem was that this one was directing all the traffic coming along the A606 into the pub car park, where most drivers turned round and drove back onto the road to continue their journey.

As I got closer to this 'French policeman', I should have guessed that this situation had something to do with my family. There was my Uncle Tony in the middle of the road obviously determined to draw in more guests! The most worrying start to my evening was that he was likely to get run over – and also, why were British drivers taking orders from a man dressed as a French policeman who was two hundred miles away from his area of jurisdiction?

Even though I had to wait until the traffic approaching from the opposite direction had turned in, I made sure to smile and wave vigorously at this happy gendarme for fear of being arrested for not being in the party mood!

As I drove into the car park, I saw an enormous marquee with lots of French-looking people loitering around and more coming and going from the pub's back door. To say that I was surprised and confused would be an understatement. From my uncle's presence, I assumed that I was in the correct place for the party Dad had invited me to – but what was all the dressing up about? And why were so many berets adorning so many male heads?

I parked and went in through the pub's back door to find Dad – and experienced something that no young adult should ever do. As I attempted to wade through what seemed to be a French invasion of Whitwell, a woman called my name. I stopped in my tracks, shocked at the horrific vision in front of me: it was my grandmother dressed as a French madame – and I'm not using the term to refer to a married French female but a lady who runs a brothel. If she'd been transported to a Parisian back street, she'd have fitted in with no problem.

I was so shocked that I was completely lost for words; what words can be used when you're confronted by your seventy-year-old grandmother dressed as a French tart? All I could muster was, 'You look … different.'

Then, just as I thought things could not get worse, my grandfather appeared dressed as a French playboy – or her pimp!

I decided the best ploy was to promise to spend time with them later and move on in case anyone saw me and thought I was related to them. Desperately needing an explanation of the trauma I had just endured, I focused on finding Dad.

I fought my way through more onion sellers than I would ever want to encounter in one place before finding him dressed as a French sailor, propping up the bar in the marquee. At least he was more sensibly attired than the rest of my family.

I realised that there was no point asking him the question that had been on the tip of my tongue since I arrived: 'Why did you not tell me it was fancy dress?' Fortunately there were others in attendance who had either missed the 'come in fancy dress' part of the invitation or who were not prepared to push out *le bateau* quite so far.

The party was in full swing with everyone fully embracing the French theme; nobody seemed bothered that neither Monsieur Chirac nor a Parisian delegation were in attendance. In fact I suspect there was a louder roar than Monsieur Chirac would have received when the local French teacher stepped forward to officially announce the twinning of these two great places.

Official business out of the way, the party upped a level. Having got used to seeing my tarty grandparents mooching around, I grabbed a glass of wine and fully embraced the celebration.

Suddenly there was a bit of a kerfuffle but standing on the periphery of the crowd I couldn't see what it was about. After a few seconds I felt a tap on my shoulder and turned to face a bunch of onions that seemed to have a face amongst them, though it was not one I recognised.

'Is that your Dad up there?' the onion man asked, pointing towards the roof of the marquee.

My eyes followed the direction of his index finger and came upon the backsides of two men, each at the top of one of the two main poles that were holding up the marquee. On closer inspection, I saw that the bottom of the man clinging to the top of the pole furthest from me looked remarkably familiar. As both the men began their descent, I realised that it was recognisable because it belonged to Dad.

I reluctantly admitted that I knew at least one of the marquee mountaineers although, to protect the tiny bit of street credibility I had left, I managed to divert the conversation to another topic before Onion Man had chance to ask me if we were related.

This unplanned and impulsive bit of mountaineering was the result of a conversation about sporting pursuits Dad had been having with his friend, who was another of the Whitwell Twinning Committee. They were discussing what sports they felt they were still fit enough to pursue. Obviously their claims were rather exaggerated having been fuelled by too many glasses of French red wine, so I suppose they were lucky the only thing that tested them was climbing the marquee poles!

Watching them descend very gradually and very carefully so as not to get splinters in delicate areas of their anatomy was the funniest thing I saw all evening. Once their feet were planted firmly on *terra firma*, Dad was crowned supreme champion of the inaugural (and as it turned out the only) Whitwell Pole Climbing Championship.

He was very proud of his achievement; mind you, he was dressed as a nineteenth-century French sailor so shinning up poles (or ships' masts) should have been something he was good at, though I doubt he'd considered that when he was choosing his outfit for the evening!

A plaque to mark the twinning was unveiled on the wall of *le pissoir* that evening, but that wasn't enough to make others (Stamford) aware of Whitwell's new status. Some weeks later, after the hangovers had subsided, there was an impromptu committee meeting to go over the recent events and, more importantly, how they had elevated Whitwell's standing when compared to Stamford.

The consensus was that more was needed to advertise the twinning and there was only one way forward: to have some road signs made that said 'Twinned with Paris'. These would be placed beneath the village signs and make it clear to anyone who passed through that this tiny Rutland village was twinned with the capital of France.

This unofficial relationship generated more media interest than anyone could have imagined, and reports appeared in many national and international newspapers. According to Dad, a short while after the surge of publicity the committee received a letter from the Parisian mayor's office, signed by Monsieur Chirac himself. It stated that although Paris would only be twinned with Rome, he agreed to the unofficial twinning with the mighty Whitwell. Mission accomplished!

This letter may have been sent – or it might have been one of Dad's very tall stories. That was definitely a habit he'd inherited from his father; as a child, teenager and adult I suffered many, many times from similar stories from both my dad and granddad, and to this day I don't know whether they were true or not. But even if it were true, I don't think all that publicity (or the real/fake letter) generated a sudden upsurge in French visitors to view the historic village their capital city was twinned with, or even to sample the local ale served in The Noel Arms.

The local council played their part in trying to keep the number of tourists to a manageable level by removing the signs, but each time they did so a member of the committee put up new ones. This game of cat and mouse continued for a while until the council finally gave in; the signs remain to remind the residents of Stamford of just how much posher Whitwell really is – and to capture the attention of any random French tourists passing through!

◻◻◻

Dad got great satisfaction from all the leg-pulling that he inflicted on his three boys but he didn't realise what an excellent teacher he was, so we all learned very quickly. This led to occasions when the boot was firmly on the other foot; sometimes Dad wasn't sure whether the words coming out of my mouth were fabricated or the absolute truth.

One such instance occurred when I was five. Stephen had been at school for two years and I had started primary school a few months before. When Dad returned from work, he often asked what had happened at school that day. Generally he started with whichever son was closest to him and on this occasion it was my older brother. His teacher had been talking to the class about what was involved in the different jobs that their parents and other adults had.

I continued to play with the Lego I had strewn over the lounge floor and wasn't really listening, but Dad seemed keen to include me in the conversation he was having with Stephen.

I was unexpectedly dragged away from the Lego by one simple question: 'Nicholas, what would you like to be when you grow up?'

It was a sensible question from a parent to a child twice my age but, as it turned out, a dangerous one to someone so young who was much keener on playing with Lego than worrying about what their future career. But I was a good boy and, as Dad had asked me, I gave his question the time and the thought it deserved and replied in a split second with the obvious answer: 'An elephant'.

He had asked and I had answered, but I have to say

that the comment that followed was hard for a five-year-old boy, who'd spent all his years on this planet wanting to be an African elephant, to process.

'No, Nicholas, you can't be an elephant.' Dad seemed pained when he spoke, and he was biting his bottom lip. 'Elephants live in Africa or India, and it's not possible because you live in England.'

I suppose this explanation was as complex as he was prepared to give to his young son; obviously a dive into Charles Darwin's Theory of Evolution would have been a step too far for a five year old. Looking back, I'm pleased he took the route he did.

Nevertheless, he decided not to leave it there and continued, 'So if you can't be an elephant, what else would you like to be when you grow up?'

In my naivety I'd thought that having one employment aspiration was enough, but now I was being told that I needed a back-up plan. This didn't throw me; as everyone knew, adults included, there was only one answer. 'A house.'

Having fulfilled my obligation to answer a father's question I was pleased with both my replies, but the second one really did stump him. He looked a bit befuddled before saying the only thing he could in such a situation: 'Fantastic.'

Somewhat worried by what he had unleashed on the world, he returned to his conversation with my older brother while I, more than happy with my contribution, returned to my mammoth Lego project.

In the years that followed Dad gave me plenty of advice and encouragement as I decided on my career path but, unsurprisingly, he never again asked me what I wanted to be when I grew up.

He usually had a knack of saying exactly the right thing at exactly the right time but, as is sometimes the case with this type of person, he sometimes got it wrong. One occasion was during his early years of filming for *Gardeners' World* when he was still a bit wet behind the ears.

When they filmed with three cameras and a large crew, the film was edited on site in one of the two lorries that also came. As was always the case, they arrived on Monday morning to shoot two consecutive programmes in three days, the first for broadcasting on the Friday of that week and the second for the following Friday.

They only came once a fortnight and, at the end of each programme, Dad often liked to mention one or two jobs he'd be doing on the following week's show. That was fine when they were filming the first of the two programmes, but it could be hazardous at the end of the second programme. A lot can happen in ten days.

The first time there was a problem was during some winter filming from Dad's front garden at the original Barnsdale. It was the end of January, and an archetypal beautiful winter's day; there was a nip in the air to remind you that it was midwinter but not a cloud in the sky, and the sun's rays were not only lighting up his beautiful winter garden, they also had some warmth in them. It was the type of day that made Dad's heart sing and he was very keen to let his viewers know this.

On Tuesday afternoon, the cameras were all set up to film the opening for the following week's programme. Everyone was in position so John Kenyon gave Dad the signal to start and off he went.

'What a glorious day this is, and what a glorious spell of weather we've been having. It's the perfect weather to pull on a jumper and get out into the garden to catch up with all those jobs that need doing. Bearing in mind how wet it's been, there are lots of things that we need to be getting on with before spring bursts forth.'

Once he had completed his exuberant outburst, he went on more sedately to talk about and demonstrate what needed to be done. It was a perfect piece and, most importantly, John Kenyon was happy, knowing how well it would come across in a week and a half's time.

For the rest of that day and most of Wednesday, they completed the filming at Barnsdale, all of which consisted of indoor jobs in Dad's greenhouse. Fast forward a week and a half and winter had returned – with a vengeance! Millions of viewers were sitting in front of their televisions ready for the start of their favourite programme, heating on full blast, cosy in their front rooms while the elements raged outside.

The music began and there Dad was, standing proudly in his front garden with a beaming smile in just a shirt and jumper. The sun was beating down and he was extolling the virtues of getting out into your garden during this fabulous weather.

The problem was that in the period between filming and broadcasting a deep blanket of snow had covered the country, so it was difficult to get out of your house let alone into your garden. There must have been millions of viewers watching Dad's excited performance and wondering what an earth this madman was talking about! He learned a very valuable lesson that day and never repeated his mistake – although there would still be a good few different mistakes.

When filming two weeks earlier, he had mentioned that he would be sowing grass seed in the following week's programme. Nothing seemed odd about this statement: it was the right time to do the job, the wrong time of year for snow, and he had a patch of bare grass that needed re-sowing, so it was the perfect scenario for both Dad and the viewer.

The problem arose when John decided that he wanted to film other jobs for that week's programme first and leave the grass sowing until the following day when conditions would be better. There had been heavy rain on Sunday night, rendering the ground too wet to prepare for sowing, but, having checked the forecast for the next two days of filming, John was confident it would definitely be fine and dry on Monday and Tuesday and therefore perfect for both grass sowing and filming.

You'd have thought that John would have been aware

of the vagaries of the British weather and the somewhat erratic weather forecasting that accompanied it, but he was full of confidence. The forecast for Monday turned out to be spot on and filming went without a hitch in perfectly dry and sunny weather. Better still, the area needed for the demonstration of preparing ground and sowing grass seed had dried out perfectly. Everything was ready for filming first thing on Tuesday morning, so on Monday evening everyone was in a buoyant mood and looking forward to the next day.

The trouble with predictions is that is what they are: an idea about what might happen. In this particular case, the forecast could not have been further from the truth. On Monday night the heavens opened with a downpour of biblical proportions that soaked the patch of bare ground that had dried out the previous day.

Although the rain was easing, it was still falling when John and the crew arrived on Tuesday morning. Those buoyant figures of the previous day now looked very down-in-the-mouth; not only could they not film the piece about sowing grass seed, they were having to work outside in the rain.

John took the executive decision that they would delay the grass sowing by a day and film it on Wednesday; instead they ploughed on with filming for the next programme to be broadcast a week later.

The rain, however, was not synchronised with the BBC filming agenda; it continued to fall all through Tuesday, eased in the night but came back again on

Wednesday. This left John with no option but to seek other ways to get this vital piece of filming done. He seemed to have forgotten that the weather forecast for Tuesday had been incorrect and noted optimistically that Thursday and Friday were due to be dry.

He and Dad hatched a plan: they would abandon any thoughts of filming sowing grass seed, leave the ground to dry on Thursday, then John would drive to Barnsdale first thing on Friday morning with a camera and sound person, film this short insert and dash back to Birmingham to get it edited and into that night's programme.

On paper the plan was perfect, but perfect plans – as they had already experienced during the week – have a tendency to get wet and soggy.

Thursday morning arrived. When Dad opened his curtains, to his amazement he saw that the weather forecasters had been right: the sun's rays were strong and warming and there wasn't a cloud in the sky. It only took the morning to dry out the piece of ground, so he decided to prepare some of it to make the next day's filming easier.

It was all going to plan. John and his colleagues and equipment arrived at 8.30am on Friday morning, having experienced no hold-ups during their drive from Birmingham. The four of them that Friday morning were like children let loose in a sweet shop with no parents present; their excitement was palpable.

They finished before lunch and, for the first time ever,

John declined Dad's offer of bread and cheese for lunch. He and his team leapt into the car and sped off towards Birmingham and the editing suite. The programme editor had already been primed as to where the section needed to be inserted and how long it should be, so John handed over the canister of film and left him to it.

He phoned Dad to let him know that their morning exertions had been worthwhile; the section had been edited into the programme and was ready to go. Safe in that knowledge, Dad settled himself in his comfy armchair in front of his television as he always did, cup of coffee in hand, just in time for the *Gardeners' World* introductory music.

He thoroughly enjoyed the first twenty minutes, then the time came to sit back and enjoy the grass-sowing sequence. He was confident that, even though it had proved difficult to film, the finished product would be as well executed as the segments he had just watched.

Television can sometimes distort the view, making things look bigger, smaller or a lot better than they actually are, and this was definitely the case with Dad's soil. As he cultivated and prepared it to sow the grass seed, it looked perfectly friable to the viewer and there was no hint that it had been a bog just a couple of days before.

The picture cut to a shot of Dad's legs, showing his feet spaced apart while he was talking about the rate of seed per square foot (he was 'old school' and not yet totally metric). He said that some people put out lines to get an accurate rate of seed sown, but with grass seed there was no need to be so accurate; an approximation was good enough.

Remembering how difficult this had been to film, he was over the moon with how it was turning out – but then he spoke the unforgettable words. Neither he nor the viewers could see his head but they could hear him loudly and clearly as he said, 'I don't bother with lines because a rough idea is fine, and as you can see I've got two foot between my legs.'

Eyes wide and mouth open with shock, he stared at the television screen which was displaying his nicely cultivated soil and the bottom half of his body, legs apart as a measure for seed sowing.

How could this faux pas have happened? All he could think to do was to phone John immediately and apologise for what was very much non-BBC language on a pre-watershed, prime-time programme. He was in panic mode and this led to an irrational fear that his position on *Gardeners' World* might be in jeopardy.

When John eventually answered his phone call, Dad launched into his apology but very quickly realised that John was not really listening because he was desperately trying to suppress his hysterical laughter. Once that had subsided, John assured him that there was nothing to worry about with regard to the BBC reaction. That massively eased Dad's fears about his position but did nothing to ease his embarrassment!

It turned out that the BBC top brass made no

comment; it seemed as if Dad had got away with that one – but afterwards he promised himself that he would watch every edit before it went off to Birmingham, just in case!

Chapter Eight

When I look at life in general it seems that like attracts like, so as I write about the funny or unusual things that happened to Dad it doesn't surprise me that there were so many. He spent his life looking for ways to create funny situations or highlight what he thought was amusing that others may have missed. He was bound to collect other incidents he wasn't looking for along the way.

My grandparents, Rosie and Cyril, had a boat; it wasn't a sea-faring vessel, just a little motorised boat that they kept on the River Nene, although to us young children it always seemed like a ship fit for sailing up the Amazon. We often spent weekends tootling up and down the river and, when the time was right, we were allowed to dive off the boat and swim.

I can't speak for my two brothers, but this escapade made me feel like Tarzan diving into a river and cutting through a tropical jungle somewhere in Africa to fight crocodiles for no apparent reason. This sort of activity was all we needed when we were younger, but as we headed towards our teenage years we were each given a fishing rod as either a birthday or Christmas present so we could fish from various points around the boat.

On this particular occasion Dad joined us and his parents for a day's boating and fishing on the River Nene. We knew that Cyril was in charge of operating the boat because, as he always did, he'd donned his sea captain's hat.

He steered the vessel along the river until we reached a point deemed suitable for lunch and a bit of fishing. Cyril brought the boat to a stop and dropped the anchor and, while we waited for Rosie to prepare the feast that was to be lunch, we each found a fishing position. Stephen was up front, fishing directly off bow (the pointy bit at the front), while Christopher and I were situated at each corner of the stern (the flat bit at the back).

We were float fishing. Having cast off, we were eagerly watching our buoyant floats and waiting patiently for the first bite. Dad was in pole position, standing in the doorway to the lower deck talking to Cyril who, being the captain, was still sitting in the driver's seat.

I'd been fishing for about a year but Christopher was a relative novice having only had his new rod for about three months, but in that short space of time he had developed a casting-off method all of his own. Rather than picking the spot in the water where he thought it was likely the fish were hiding (as we professional fishermen did), his objective was to project his float as far as he possibly could. When we were fishing from a river bank, the momentum created by the force he used often propelled him a step forward, which was fine as long as he was standing back from the water's edge.

There was an occasion when we were fishing on the banks of Thrapston Reservoir when he was concentrating so hard on his casting out that he didn't realise that each time he took a step forward. It was only when the top of his wellies were below water level that he noticed!

He didn't learn his lesson, though, and continued to employ this technique – including on this occasion when he was fishing from the back of his grandparents' boat. Keeping the forward momentum of his legs under control, he cast and waited for a bite; when he didn't get one, he decided to cast out again but in a different direction, and further.

He gave it everything he had and, out of the corner of my eye, I saw him disappear over the edge of the boat! It was only when he heard the almighty splash that Dad realised someone had gone in – and it came as no surprise that it was Christopher.

Dad immediately broke off his conversation with Cyril, rushed to the back of the boat and peered over the edge just as Christopher's head came bursting up out of the water, spluttering as he tried to wipe the water from his eyes. Obviously I was doing the concerned, brotherly thing and clutching my sides as I crumpled in a heap and laughed hysterically. Stephen, the other caring brother, must have heard the commotion but he carried on fishing.

Dad waited a few seconds because Christopher seemed to be in shock – although he was the only person shocked that he was the one who'd fallen in the water – then asked Christopher if he was still holding his fishing rod. No: he must have let go of it as he hit the water. With that explanation out of the way and the rod a goner, Christopher was glad to see Dad extend his arm in a gesture that indicated he would help him back onto the boat.

However, there was a reason that Dad had made us place the fishing hook not far beneath the float: the River Nene was quite shallow at that point and when Christopher hurled himself into the river he did so with a bellyflop. Although totally submerged, he had stayed fairly close to the surface. He had no real idea of the depth of the river because, being a youngster, he was only short and his feet didn't quite touch the river bottom.

A very grateful Christopher saw Dad's extended arm and he stretched out his own right arm. Then, to his great surprise, Dad's hand sailed past his and came to rest on the top of his head. He heard the following words: 'Well, you'd better go back down and get it then!' just before the life-saving hand pushed him back under the water.

This only made me laugh harder as my younger brother disappeared again. About ten seconds later, we were treated to a scene from the legend of King Arthur: a fishing rod clutched in a small hand at the end of an arm suddenly appeared from beneath the surface and seemed to be held for a second or two before the rest of Christopher re-emerged from the depths of the river.

After retrieving his rod, my brother was left to tread water for a while, but only because it took Dad about thirty seconds to stop laughing enough to yank his son back onto the boat. Apparently, at the beginning of the 1970s this was deemed normal parental behaviour so any witnesses wouldn't have thought about contacting Social Services!

Rosie appeared; having finished preparing lunch, she dried off her young grandson and gave him the change of clothes Dad had cunningly packed in full knowledge that a drenching was inevitable. We tucked into the magnificent buffet and Christopher joined the feast – though he seemed rather keen to avoid any fish-related sandwiches!

This flow of funny events continued unabated, and during a trip to New Orleans Dad found one of his best. He and Lynda had flown out to enjoy two weeks of southern US culture and music and had hired a car. Dad did all the driving and found that the hardest part was not that the cars had the steering wheel on the wrong side and there were exits on both sides of the freeway, but that the speed limit was much lower than in the UK. Managing to keep his accelerator foot under control had been a problem all his driving life – although he was more conscious of his speed in America because the police carry guns!

In the week and a half they travelled around New Orleans and Louisiana, there were no driving malfunctions and Dad seemed to get to grips with exiting the freeways from either side. After a several days exploring New Orleans, they decided to take in some country air and headed out of the city on the freeway towards the open countryside. Dad was in the driver's seat and Lynda was in charge of navigation.

Passing through the outer limits of the city, they felt the air becoming cleaner as pockets of open country appeared around them. Lynda had a road map open on her lap and was passing instructions to Dad, but moments after she'd told him to take the second exit on the left he suddenly turned the steering wheel left onto the next slip road.

This was the last thing she expected. As he ground to a halt in a layby, she asked why he'd taken the first exit when she'd said they needed the second one. His explanation was simple: apparently – and unnoticed by Lynda – they'd just passed the funniest sign he'd ever seen and he was determined to get a picture of it.

Lynda's only concern was that he intended walking down the edge of the freeway with his camera and dodging the traffic as it hurtled by. However, Dad had an even dafter idea. His simple plan involved them swapping places, driving round in a loop to re-join the freeway before the sign, so that when they passed it again he could lean out of the window to photograph it.

This meant that Lynda would have to drive very

carefully and very slowly on a fast freeway. To him this idea seemed reasonably easy to execute, but it was daft for two reasons: firstly, Dad was doing all the driving as Lynda did not feel confident driving on wide, unfamiliar American freeways; and secondly, it was a twenty-mile drive to get back to the sign! Dad was undaunted; the first problem he felt he could overcome, and once Lynda saw the funny sign he was sure she'd agree that the distance was well worth the end result.

To keep this excited fifty-six-year-old man happy, Lynda agreed to drive. Off they went with Dad now in charge of the map, though it soon emerged that his map-reading skills were nowhere near as good as Lynda's. Even so, they eventually found their way back onto the freeway only ten miles further down than they'd planned.

As they closed in on the sign, Dad rested his SLR camera on the window frame of the window, which he'd opened the minute they had set off – just in case. This was a once-in-a-lifetime opportunity because he knew he wouldn't be able to persuade Lynda to do the circuit again.

Suddenly there was the sign in the distance. He leaned forward settled into position, pressed the viewfinder against his eye and held his index finger over the shutter button. Lynda was concentrating so hard on the road and her speedometer that she didn't see the sign, but she was happy to hear several clicks of the camera shutter. Their strange mission had been accomplished!

When they were past it Lynda pulled off the freeway at the same junction as before, happy to relinquish the driving to the child-like adult sitting next to her who looked like the cat who'd just been delivered the largest pot of cream ever!

When they resumed their journey, Dad was keen to hear that Lynda had understood his need to come back and take a picture for posterity, so he was a bit deflated when she revealed she'd missed seeing it the second time too. He decided to do what no sane person should and describe it to her. His SLR camera was not digital so they wouldn't see the photographs until they were back in the UK; all his detailed explanation did was to give away the punchline before Lynda actually saw the sign.

If nothing else, his explanation was detailed. The large, red-painted sign showed the head and shoulders of a man and with large words forming the briefest of sentences, *The Crab Man*, surrounded by pictures of fish, lobsters, prawns and other sea-life that he obviously sold. Taking pride of place in the middle of the sign was a large picture of a crab. Then – and this was the reason for the whole detour – in the top right-hand corner on a blue background were the loud and proud words in the brightest white: Surprise her with crabs!

This sign increased Dad's pleasure in his American jaunt tenfold, even more so when he received the developed photograph. Lynda finally understood the reason for the diversion and, albeit somewhat late, agreed that it had indeed been worth it.

Having done the rounds of all his friends and family, the picture eventually took pride of place on the cork board in their downstairs toilet. Dad had erected this board as somewhere to pin the things he thought funny: odd letters sent to him by viewers; letters sent to other presenters (there was a very strange one sent to a female presenter); clips from newspapers or magazines that he found funny (the Colemanballs section in *Private Eye* occupied several spaces), and anything funny that was related to him. One of the first newspaper articles to adorn the board was *The Worst Dressed Duo on TV* newspaper clipping, but this had to fight for the attention of anyone using the downstairs loo because his 'Crab Man' photo now took pride of place.

One picture that was missing from the cork board, but a favourite all the same, was that of a pooing hippopotamus. An unusual topic, I grant you, but a picture Dad was keen to show one and all on his return from Kenya where they had been visiting an old work colleague of Lynda's. This picture had been taken on a mini safari. By his own admission, it was the best he had taken during the trip, even though he'd got through four rolls of film, each with thirty-six exposures, photographing a whole host of African wildlife.

Dad and Lynda stayed for two weeks. Not long after their return I popped up to see them aware that I would get the usual short holiday debrief, but this time it was different. On the kitchen table was a wad of photographs waiting to be gone through one by one.

In order to make sure the full comedic effect of his best photograph was appreciated he'd put it at the bottom of the pile so it could be accompanied by a full and detailed explanation. The picture consisted of a soil bank with tufts of grass growing sporadically across the top and a beautiful, clear blue sky beyond, but it was spoilt by the large number of dirt specks all over the picture.

It seemed an odd photo amongst more than a hundred pictures of Kenyan wildlife roaming the plain because there was nothing of any significance. I had seen impala, elephant, giraffe, lion, crocodile, baboon, warthog and the like, but this one had none of those. Was it the sky, the bank or the grass he'd been photographing? And if so, why was it interesting?

I was struggling to see any point to this picture and was even more confused when Dad enthusiastically asked me if I could see it? See what? It was just sky and a few tufts of grass taken through a dirty lens. I started to wonder if he had finally lost the plot.

He pointed enthusiastically at the specks of dirt on the blue sky and asked if I knew what they were and what animal they had come from. Eventually we were starting to get somewhere. Apparently there was an animal not in view on the other side of the bank, but I had no idea what it was or what relationship the specks of dirt bore to it.

Dad was ramping up the tension and his own excitement as he headed towards his punchline. He explained that the specks had come from a hippopotamus and that, incredibly, they were its poo. It was all about nature having created something wonderful – not that hippo poo is wonderful, but Dad thought that the way they dispense it is. He had obviously been told about this by his hosts and he was keen to explain his newfound knowledge to his middle son, like it or not.

Apparently, because the hippo spends most of the day virtually submerged in water, they don't defecate next to themselves. Instead, when they need to evacuate their bowels they raise themselves from the water (or more precisely their back ends) while their short tail spins like the blade of a helicopter. (At this point, Dad was as excited as a six-year-old.) This spreads the manure far and wide in minute quantities and it dissipates in the water.

He explained the educational and humorous quality of the photograph – and I learned a valuable lesson about defecating hippos that would stand me in good stead for the rest of my life!

The days of taking pictures with an SLR film camera, as opposed to the modern digital ones, were interesting for Dad both when he was the editor of *Practical Gardening* magazine and when he was writing books. Pictures were taken without knowing if they would be suitable until they had been developed. Dad stayed close to home for this job and employed my older brother Steve to take pictures; after all, Steve was a professional photographer and he eventually worked solely for Dad.

Steve got through hundreds of reels of film a year, all of which needed to be professionally developed within a day. Dad enjoyed the many benefits of living a rural life but having a professional film developer on your doorstep was not one of them, so Steve had to travel to and from Leicester to get the films processed. Once they were developed and back at Barnsdale, he went through them meticulously so he could present the best ones to Dad for his final approval before they were sent to the appropriate publication or publisher.

On one particular occasion they had both been in the garden taking pictures for the book *Geoff Hamilton's Cottage Gardens* before Steve dashed to Leicester to put them in for processing. The deadline to get the pictures to the publisher was tight, primarily because the weather had been poor and taking them had been delayed by several days.

This was compounded by a problem at the film processing company, which delayed the negatives even more. Dad phoned the publisher to say that the pictures would be a bit late arriving, and at that point I went into his office to ask him something. He was concentrating so hard on the call that he didn't notice me sneak into the office behind him.

What happened next must have popped into his head mid-conversation made it clear that genetically I stood no chance!

As a child I had always enjoyed the Disney cartoon film *Snow White and the Seven Dwarfs*; to this day I hold it and its songs in great affection as a piece of creative genius. Now, I thought I'd managed to get into the office without Dad hearing me but, having replaced the phone receiver, he swung round on his chair and belted out: 'Someday my prints will come!'

Having listened to part of his telephone conversation I was aware of the delay with the latest batch of pictures, but unprepared for this outburst. It illustrated perfectly how quick witted he was – and also that he was a very strange man! All too often it was impossible to understand how his thought processes worked, how he got from a starting point to a conclusion – and why the conclusion ended up being so odd, albeit almost always very funny!

There is no better example of this than what happened during one of my daily visits to see Dad. I usually went at the end of my working day while he was still in his office finishing an article or writing another book. It was two weeks before Christmas and I'd had a relatively quiet day at the nursery, but that had given me the opportunity to finish checking the 1996 Barnsdale plants' mail-order catalogue and get it to our local printer. All the people who had ordered plants during 1995 were getting a free catalogue and I liked to send it out so that they received it around mid-January, so getting it to the printer before Christmas was essential. It was a fairly laborious task sitting at the computer and reading slowly through to make sure I caught any mistakes rather than reading what I thought should be there.

The combination of having almost nobody to talk to and staring at a computer screen all day had left me looking forward more than usual to my chat with Dad. I locked up and tootled next door to his office; he was where I expected him to be at his desk, but not at his computer. He was clearly concentrating very hard, with a pair of scissors in one hand and what looked like a piece of card in the other, slowly and carefully cutting away.

As I approached I saw that he was holding a Christmas card and cutting through the picture at the front. How very odd, I thought.

I asked him what he was doing and he replied that he was sending it to Steve Pink. This name will mean nothing to most people, but to Dad he was a very important person indeed; Steve was his agent and therefore responsible for getting him work that generated the income he needed to keep Barnsdale going. Obviously Steve didn't work for free and took ten percent commission on all the paid work he organised for Dad.

Knowing that Dad was sending this mutilated Christmas card to Steve still made no sense to me. He seemed to be cutting out a circular segment: was he sending the bit he was cutting out, or was he cutting out something he didn't like and sending Steve the rest of the card? The only way to find out was to ask, so I did.

I am chuckling as I type this because, to me, this was one of the funniest and cleverest thoughts I can remember Dad having and perfectly sums up his sense of humour. With the widest grin on his face he replied, 'Well, I thought that as he gets ten percent of everything else, I would send him ten percent of a Christmas card.'

I'm absolutely positive that none of Steve's other clients ever put so much thought into the card they sent him – and none that gave the sender a smile that lasted through Christmas and beyond.

At the time I thought his next trick was fairly unique, thought up by Dad with no help from his agent as a means of making a bit more money, but over the years it emerged that this is something far too many authors carry out. I was used to his wacky ideas that involved not just himself but family members too, sometimes of their own free will and sometimes after he'd cajoled them.

Writing was something Dad was very good at, writing books in particular; he enjoyed it and fortunately it generated a reasonable income. He used the money to fund his garden – and what a garden it was, packed full of brilliant ideas for gardeners because of the way he had laid it out and what he had created within it.

The problem was that with this massive positive came a massive negative. Creating a garden full of ideas for viewers came at a cost and was labour intensive, so all the money he generated from book sales was gratefully received.

To maximise his book sales, Dad was determined to make sure they were always at the forefront of the book buyers' minds when they entered a shop. Whenever he was in a town or city and had a few minutes to spare, he'd visit booksellers such as WH Smiths and Waterstones and go in with one thing on his mind – and that was not to buy books. Looking his most innocent, he would rearrange the displays so that his books were facing outwards at the front of the shelves so they were the first to be seen by a potential purchaser. Once he'd completed the dirty deed, he left in as innocent a manner as he had entered.

I found it hilarious – not just his innocent-looking his entry and exit but that he thought it would make a difference. However, hearing about this odd activity seemed to infect me like a virus and before long I was also diverting into bookshops and doing the same thing, taking great pride in my achievement of leaving the shop without having been spotted just like Dad.

However there were occasions when, as an author, being spotted was beneficial. Such an occurrence happened in W H Smith, not on a high street but in a motorway service station concession. Dad had stopped to refuel (not his car but himself) and buy his daily newspaper, which is why he found himself face to face with a cashier. It was rare for him not to have some cash in his pocket, but on this occasion he only had his cheque book.

That was fine, except that the cheque book fell into

the part of Dad's brain that stored all of the things he wanted to keep that had not moved into the 'new age'. In fact, he kept the cheque book next to his typewriter for that very reason, meaning that he did not have his new and, in his view, un-necessary cheque guarantee card.

When he went to pay by cheque, the cashier asked for his guarantee card. When he said he didn't have one, she followed company policy by informing him that she could not accept a cheque without the card.

For Dad this was not how this small, seemingly simple transaction should pan out. Having argued his case unsuccessfully for a while, he had another idea. He told the cashier that he would return in a few seconds and disappeared into the magazine and books' section of the shop, returning with a copy of *Geoff Hamilton's Cottage Gardens*. He turned it over and showed her his picture on the back cover. Apparently, and I am not sure if this is company policy, being the author of a book in stock in W H Smith is as good as a cheque guarantee card.

When he recounted this story to me, I said that she may have been able to see that he was an author but how did she know he was an author with money? The only response I got was that grin he gave when he knew that he had got away with something – and the same thing was never likely to happen again.

Chapter Nine

At its peak *Gardeners' World* was shown on BBC2 every Friday for fifty weeks of the year. This was like heaven to Dad because it gave him the opportunity to educate and inform his viewers on all the jobs that needed doing year-round in the garden.

There was always going to be a downside to this but it was certainly not something that would get the better of Dad.

To ensure there was at least one veg-based sequence in every programme, he had created the 'allotment' where he could grow enough to satisfy this weekly demand but keep it to a manageable size. To achieve this he had to 'bolt-on' veg-growing areas to the side of his allotment as well as growing in an identical space opposite. The clever bit was to never show the whole area but focus on the allotment and use the other areas as small, individual spaces.

Even with all this space, he didn't grow vast quantities of produce; instead he filled it with as many different veg varieties as possible. The mantra at Barnsdale was just the same as any allotmenteer's space, 'grow to eat';

growing what was needed not only saved waste but made the best use of the available space.

He still needed to be clever in order to fill his weekly requirement, which is why he often used techniques such as the one he had for beetroot. Rather than sowing one type of beetroot, which wouldn't give him much to show, he sowed six, using varieties such as the good old reliable Boltardy as well as Burpees Golden, Choggia Pink, Cylindrica, Bulls Blood and Moneta.

Those who grow beetroot know that Boltardy is a reliable and tasty variety, tried and tested for more than fifty years, and is the go-to variety for many gardeners, so this was the first one on Dad's list. However, showing how to sow beetroot was a task that could only be done once, irrespective of how many varieties were sown, because the method is the same for almost all of them. I say 'almost all' because sowing Moneta would have filled a weekly veg slot, as being a monogerm type, this variety can also be used for the 'multi-sowing' method, which is also suitable for veg such as carrots, kohl rabi, parsnip, onions, leeks, pak choi and turnips.

Having filled two weeks of veg-based instruction on *Gardeners' World* with beetroot, Dad was well on his way but not yet finished. There was the potential to fill another five programmes when growing the yellow-fleshed Burpees Golden, the white-and-pink ringed Choggia Pink, the long, thin version Cylindrica, Bulls Blood (where you can eat the root as well as using the leaves as a substitute for spinach) and his multi-sown

Moneta. Each of these varieties would be compared with Boltardy, which was the 'control' variety.

In this way he could fill the veg slot in each programme for seven weeks and complete more than an eighth of what was required for a full year's worth of gardening inserts – all with one type of veg!

Not satisfied with filling that volume of programmes, Dad wanted to do more. He approached John Kenyon with what he told him was 'an excellent idea': he wanted to start running trials, not criminal ones but those involving vegetables. John thought the principle was a good one but struggled to imagine the format, how Dad would stretch this over so many programmes and how he'd keep the viewers interested.

Unwittingly Dad was certain that it had been their evening in the Noel Arms that persuaded John to take him on as a presenter, so a similar night might persuade him about this fantastic idea. With the passing of time he suspected that he might have to ramp up the offering, so decided that a pint with a meal was the probably the only way he'd get what he wanted. Unsurprisingly, John didn't resist the offer.

John's first question was about the type of vegetable Dad would feature; as this would be the first trial, it should be something commonly grown. Dad said that he would start with tomatoes; everyone knew what a tomato was and lots of viewers grew them both inside glasshouses and outside in their veg plots. With several different growing techniques and lots of varieties to choose from, they were the perfect fruiting vegetable to kick off the trials.

With his mouth full of steak and ale pie, John nodded agreement. Even though his own food was going cold, Dad started explaining how the trial would work from when the seeds were sown, to how well they germinated and grew on, to the health and quality of the mature plants, through to how well they cropped and – the *pièce de resistance* – how good the flavour was. Once fruiting, there would be a harvesting session twice a week when the fruit from each variety would be weighed and its quality assessed. It would all be professionally done but simple enough for an amateur gardener to follow. He had thought about it a lot and was very keen to follow his lifelong mantra: if a job's worth doing then it's worth doing well.

By the time he'd finished his explanation Dad was only half way through his main course whereas John had already ordered a coffee. At that point Dad realised that he had to speak less and eat faster because he had left no time for John to ask questions; now they would all come together, delaying Dad's meal even more.

To his surprise, even after being bombarded with so much information, John only had the one question: 'When are you thinking of starting?' If only Dad had known it would be that easy he'd definitely have eaten faster and spoken less because he was now confronted with more than half of a cold lasagne to finish!

Even though it was a bitterly cold January day, Dad

was still excited about his new project – so excited that he got a bit carried away when he was ordering his tomato seeds. It seemed no time at all before the postman was knocking on his door clutching a large parcel containing many different varieties of tomatoes all nicely wrapped in colourful packets.

Dad dashed straight off to the greenhouse clutching his bundle of joy and leaving his coffee to go cold on the kitchen table. Once inside, he ripped open the outer packaging, eager to see if everything he had ordered was inside. He placed the seed packets into different piles: one pile for early sowing of the indoor greenhouse varieties; one for normal sowing of indoor greenhouse types; one for varieties destined for the polythene tunnel; one for outdoor cordons; one for outdoor bush types, and one for outdoor container varieties.

As he placed each pile into its own box, he believed that he'd covered all bases. There would be at least one method of producing a crop of tomatoes to accommodate every viewer's growing area, ranging from those with a heated greenhouse right through to those who grew tomatoes on a patio or the balcony of their flat.

Content with his morning's work, he returned to the kitchen table and his cold coffee to write a sowing schedule for each tomato-growing method.

The following morning he put the plan into action and sowed the first varieties, those earlies that would be grown in the warmest greenhouse. His trials were now officially underway!

As he was being filmed sowing, he explained the idea of the trial and the basics of what he would showing viewers on a regular basis throughout the season. He promised he would leave no stone unturned to deliver the most comprehensive results ever offered to amateur gardeners. They would get to see the seedlings of this early sowing being pricked out and eventually potted on, with the staged filming being far more in depth for the first sowing than the ones that followed. He wanted his viewers to understand the importance of early sowing because these tomatoes would be the most valuable as they would be available when tomatoes were still very expensive in the shops.

The trials seemed to be progressing without a hitch and were certainly far easier than he had imagined they would be. By the first week of June the outdoor temperature had improved to the point at which he could plant his outdoor and container varieties with little fear of frost damaging them.

He now had the full complement of tomatoes on the go. The earliest varieties were already close to cropping and the other types at varying stages. Soon the first batch of tomatoes from the heated greenhouse started to ripen and we were all very glad of them; not only were they cheaper to produce than the ones in the shops, but the flavour was phenomenal and they actually tasted of tomato!

Three weeks later, the tomatoes in the barely heated, frost-free greenhouse started to crop – and it was at this point that I began to question Dad's carefully constructed plan. It reinforced what we already knew that he was an excellent tomato grower; when this new crop was added to the tomatoes he was already harvesting from the heated greenhouse, we were forced to eat tomatoes as a starter, with our main course and somehow, in one form or another, as part of our daily pudding! I love the humble tomato – but not necessarily for each course of a meal every day, and certainly not for pudding. Have *you* ever heard of a tomato meringue pie, tomato panacotta, tomato crumble or a tomato posset?

Then the tunnel varieties kicked in. Although they added colour to the mix, with yellow, plum-purple, white, stripy and even green fruit, it was the volume that caused concern. Even Dad grudgingly admitted that trying to eat what was being produced by these three growing techniques was a problem.

To get rid of the excess, he offered them to friends and family but this only made a small dent in the crop. He considered asking for hand-out from the EU for his tomato mountain, but then he thought of the perfect scenario to reduce both the tomato burden and his financial one in funding his garden. His great plan was to pay his staff in tomatoes and kill two birds with one stone! As it turned out, he was the only one who thought this was a great idea and all the staff opted for hard cash instead!

Dad really hated to waste anything, so finding a way to use the ripe tomatoes was now keeping him awake at night. Then, like a knight in shining armour, I rode to the rescue with an idea that would obliterate his tomato mountain and make sure that he got a proper night's sleep. After they had been weighed, I would take the crates of tomatoes he did not need to the nursery, bag them up and give them away to any customer who spent more than £10 on plants.

What a response I got! I'd never had such a response to any of my ideas at any point in my life before even though to me this solution seemed obvious. And I think Dad was overcome by the emotion of seeing himself waste-free.

It wasn't just Dad who was so delighted with my idea; I got the same reaction from customers who spent enough money to become eligible for a bag of juicy, tasty, fresh tomatoes to take home.

It was working really well, but then Dad's tomatoes ramped up their production to the next level. I had to follow suit and drop the level at which customers qualified for their 'bonus'. I decided to drop it to a £5 plant purchase, which was very crafty because that meant that 99% of my customers qualified for a bag of tomatoes whether they wanted them or not. That was our level of desperation, but thankfully this lower level of eligibility cleared the daily pile of tomatoes – until the outdoor ones kicked in!

I remember mentioning to Dad a few years before this tomato extravaganza that his hair looked as if it had started to thin and, to be fair, he was of that age. His combing technique to arrange what he had left became more careful, but by the time the outdoor varieties started producing ripe tomatoes all that went out of the window and he was pulling what was left of his hair out in handfuls. We were both doing what we could to offload the vast quantity of produce but it seemed that Dad would have to put up with having some wastage.

If he'd turned to his middle son earlier, his barnet would have remained much thicker. When he eventually asked for help, I came up trumps again with an extension to my original idea. I was sure that removing my £5 limit would boost the uptake of the bags of tomatoes and we started filling each bag until it was overflowing. That definitely solved Dad's tomato-induced headache, as well as preventing the removal of any more of his diminished follicles.

I was right: bags of tomatoes disappeared at an alarming rate, but just as I thought we were on the homeward straight the sun came out and the temperatures rocketed – as did the production of both the indoor and outdoor tomatoes.

In any other year, professional and amateur tomato growers would have been over the moon with this weather, but they were not in our situation and we had got to the nightmarish stage where it seemed that everywhere we turned there were tomatoes.

I was not getting enough customers into the nursery to cope so, in between persuading customers that even though they already had tomatoes in their fridge they could never have too many, I racked my brains for other ways to get rid of them. My first thought was to stand at the side of the road and hurl bags through the open windows of cars as they hurtled past the nursery entrance, but that might have got me in trouble with the local constabulary. Mind you, the insurance claims where it said 'reason for crash' would have been interesting if someone wrote 'being hit on the side of the head with a bag of tomatoes'.

The second and much safer thought was to take them on the road: I could fill my car with bags of tomatoes and give them away to the people I met when I was out and about. At that busy time of the year I went into Oakham every day to the bank, so I made sure that I had at least two full carrier bags of tomatoes to hand out. This worked well, although some people found it odd to be approached in the street by a bloke dishing out free tomatoes.

After a couple of weeks, though, I found that when people saw me coming with a full carrier bag in each hand, they crossed the road. Even the lady in the petrol station hid behind the counter when I arrived to fill my car with fuel.

I was in danger of becoming a local pariah but fortunately the clouds rolled in, the temperature dropped to a far more average British summertime level and, thankfully, so did the rate of tomato production.

As summer headed towards autumn, production tailed off to a gentle dribble and I could give away all the tomatoes by lunchtime. This whole traumatic episode happened off-camera, so the millions of *Gardeners' World* viewers were unaware of the impact the tomato trial had not just on Dad's life but mine too. It had taken definitely taken over my days as I became obsessed with only one thing: how to get rid of this over-supply of tomatoes.

The real positive of this trial was that the viewing public loved it and learned a lot from following it. From statistics obtained by the BBC, it seemed they were very enthusiastic about the results – though the statistics didn't show my delight when the trial finally came to an end.

The trial proved a raging success but for me there was a massive downside: Dad was already looking forward to the next year and the next trial. He was a man on a mission. If the next trial came even close to the tomato trauma, then I'd be packing my bags and leaving home!

As it turned out, there was no need to worry. I can't describe my relief when I stood next to Dad as John Kenyon asked him what the next trial would be and Dad replied, 'Aubergines.' What a joy: only three plants each of six varieties – I could definitely cope with that!

Although Dad chose the varieties for these trials and, as was the case with a lot of the work carried out in the gardens at Barnsdale, he did an awful lot of the work, the rest was done by one of his three paid staff members. In February 1989 I joined the team, having spent nearly six years learning my craft after completing my college diploma.

My last job had been as a propagation manager on a nursery in the Midlands, but on my first day of work I realised that I had made a terrible mistake. I loved propagating but, without really being able to put my finger on the exact reason why, it didn't feel like the right place for me.

I gave three times the amount of required notice to make sure that the nursery owner had plenty of time to find my replacement. I had no job to go to but I had a plan and, as far as I was concerned, it was definitely the best way forward. The only commitment I had was to Dennis, my cat, so this was the perfect time to move on.

I had options once I left my job in the Midlands. I could have moved back in with my mum in Kettering, but it was difficult to exert pressure on Dad when living twenty-five miles away and only seeing him occasionally. Instead, I did the only decent thing: imposed myself on him at Barnsdale on the understanding that it was a short-term arrangement.

He was clear that, much as he loved his three sons and much as he wanted to help us, once we had flown the nest we were not coming back! I'd known this since my early twenties and had the damning evidence to prove it.

This watershed moment happened in 1983 when I was still at Writtle College. On one of my few trips home, I asked Dad for a bit of extra money to buy the books I needed. Now bear in mind that I did not come home often as I was a very poor horticultural student who had no spare cash even to run the old banger his dad had bought for him.

Hearing my plea, Dad suddenly saw an opportunity to give his middle son some worldly advice. He replied, 'I am happy to give you what you've asked for, but I would like to give you the best piece of life advice anyone could give you.' Wow: there was great promise in that answer as he hadn't dismissed my request out of hand or gone through the usual rigmarole.

All through my life Dad liked to play a game; on reflection, it was a good game because it made you understand that nothing in life was easy and things were rarely given to you. If any of his children asked for something that meant he had to spend money, his reply was usually a firm 'no'.

But that was not the end of the conversation. After the initial rejection we all learned that the next stage of the game was to negotiate from 'no' to get as close to what we'd initially asked for. Unusually, on this occasion there was no need for negotiation because it seemed that all I had to do was listen and the cash would be mine – although I was certainly not ready for what he was about to say.

He continued, 'The best piece of advice I can give you is to never have children because you can't bloody well get rid of them!'

I didn't reply. What was the point? How could you reply to such a well-thought-out and well-constructed piece of fatherly wisdom? All I could do was take the money and slope off, well and truly chastised.

I made myself at home in the spare room at Barnsdale and worked for Dad in the garden with a parental contract that stated I would pay no rent and he would pay me a small allowance to run my car as long as I continued to apply for appropriate horticultural jobs. Bearing in mind it was the only option I had, I agreed and set about every garden task I was given with gusto.

I was only twenty-seven, full of energy and a desire to help and do well. As I had no money for extra-curricular activities, I worked seven days a week, which was fine because I loved what I did. Being a good boy, in order to adhere to my contract I occasionally took time off to attend job interviews. I only went to the absolute minimum to keep Dad happy and let him think that getting a job was my objective: one on the south coast (petrol paid for by Dad) and one just outside Leicester. Neither of them were what I'd have wanted if I was actually intending to find a job, but I had to show willing as I put my plan into action.

Over recent years Dad and I had spoken many times about setting up a little business, which would have been perfect for me. I'd been helping at the garden centre since I was a teenager and we'd always worked well together. My return to Barnsdale was testimony that we still did, so my cunning plan was to gradually twist his arm until he agreed to become my business partner.

I've always looked to the future and been happy to wait for something I really want, particularly if patience is needed. In this case, the softly-softly approach was certainly the way forward. I had been drip-feeding Dad ideas for my business plan in a way that it still seemed to be a long way into the future. He seemed to be encouraging and still keen that at some point we would start a new Hamilton family business.

I talked business to him more often as I ramped up the pressure – then out of the blue he announced that the walled kitchen garden on our big local landowner's estate was up for rent and he'd made an appointment for us to go and look at it! I was dumfounded, not just because he had shown no signs of wanting to move the business conversation nearer to reality but also because I hadn't realised that I had such powers of persuasion.

On the day of the viewing, I jumped into Dad's Land Rover and he drove the half a mile down the road to the old walled garden where the land agent for the estate was waiting for us, clipboard in hand. There were two reasons for using the term 'old': it had been built during the Victorian era to supply the house with fresh fruit and veg but hadn't been used for some considerable time. The other reason was its run-down state; the once-beautiful Victorian greenhouses were so dilapidated that they were literally caving in. These had been constructed with half the greenhouse underground and half above; their state was sad to see because I had worked in greenhouses like these at

Raveningham Gardens in Norfolk. Each year those had had a small amount of money spent on them for a lick of paint and minor maintenance, and they'd remained in tip-top condition. These, quite obviously, had not.

My first impression was that this enclosed area was perfect; it had plenty of land to grow perennials and shrubs for division and cuttings, as well as somewhere to grow on my potted plants for sale. There was a potting shed, a gardener's bothy and plenty of outbuildings, as well as the dilapidated greenhouses. Dad seemed keen too, primarily because he saw the chance to oust me from his house and into the gardener's bothy.

After showing us around the site, the land agent started to talk about cost. When he mentioned the annual rent, both Dad and I took a sharp intake of breath. I looked at Dad's rapidly paling face and saw that this was a deal-breaker. As if the cost of the annual rent was not sufficient, the land agent then added that the estate would expect us to renovate the greenhouses while we held the tenancy.

As soon as he'd finished speaking, Dad thanked him for his time, said we'd consider the details and one of us would come back to him in a day or two. However, as we turned to walk back to the Land Rover we both knew it was a non-starter. The rent alone would have been a massive stretch for Dad for several years until the nursery started to bring in money to pay for itself, and the added renovation work pushed the cost way beyond what we'd expected.

On the drive home not only did he give me the responsibility of phoning the land agent to pass on the bad news but, from the way he was talking, it also seemed that the whole business partnership idea was now on a back burner.

I knew that I'd have to wait a few weeks so he had time to get over this setback; I also knew that I had to make him realise that not all our possible partnership ideas would be this expensive.

Having worked at weekends and during school holidays from the age of fourteen, I had not drawn an awful lot from 'the bank of Dad' over the years, which meant that I had very little guilt about drawing from this financial institution now. The fact that Dad would also benefit was my 'Unique Selling Point' and I hoped that this USP would mask any inkling that I was merely a child sponging from a parent.

Having not mentioned any business ventures for a couple of weeks, I was completely blindsided by another surprise announcement again involving the local landowner. The previous evening Dad had been taking to a friend of his in the pub, having just popped in for a swift half, and the topic of conversation had turned to his visit to the old kitchen garden. After Dad mentioned the extraordinary costs involved, his friend said he'd heard a rumour that the landowner was looking to generate funds; he was under the impression they were looking to sell off some land. Unexpectedly, this was the information Dad needed to reignite our business plan – and with absolutely no help from me.

He returned home with a plan of his own and the following morning I was summoned to his office where he told me his fantastic new idea. He was going to phone the landowner and bypass the land agent; he felt that this direct approach was more likely to yield the result he wanted, which was to purchase the strip of land at the end of his own garden.

It was a similar sized plot to his Barnsdale garden, and had been intensively farmed for decades, but Dad felt that there was a line where it could be amputated from the larger field beyond. This line stretched from the far corner of Dad's plot to the corner of the small electricity sub-station some hundred yards away; before he even picked up the phone he knew this was correct because he'd already checked.

Although the term 'amputated' was an odd one to use when talking to the landowner, his main point would be the benefit they would receive from making the field easier to cultivate and harvest, so he was confident of a positive outcome.

Having explained everything to the landowner, he was confronted by two hurdles he'd not anticipated. Firstly, the decision was not made by the landowner but by the board of trustees that made major financial decisions. They only met twice a year but we hoped this biannual gathering would happen sooner rather than later. Secondly – and this was going to be the main hurdle – was the cost of buying the land. Having already had our fingers burned with the kitchen garden enquiry, we were not getting too excited at the prospect of this business venture taking off until the costs had come through, and we both readied ourselves for an unpleasant shock.

We had just passed midsummer day 1989 when Dad received a letter containing the good news that trustees were prepared to sell the land, exactly as marked out by Dad, and including the cost. Later that morning I was summoned to the office with no explanation as to why but, because of Dad's tone of voice, I expected the worst.

Once I was sitting down, he began to speak in a subdued tone as he reached for the letter. Everything about him seemed negative: his tone, his actions and even his down-in-the-mouth expression.

He removed the letter from its envelope and read it to me very slowly and in a very bland tone that did not change when he got to the bit where it said that we could buy the land. Instead he looked up at me and waited for the news to kick in.

I was stunned but overjoyed because the plan was well and truly back on track. It was several days later when the euphoria started to subside and I realised the one thing Dad had not mentioned was how much the land would cost. I was in no rush to find out but eventually, when I got the opportunity to broach the issue, all I was told was that it was for him to know and not something I needed to be concerned about. The closest I got to finding out was when he told me that it was not as much has he'd expected.

After Dad passed away I discovered that it was actually quite a bit higher than he'd expected; it seems that the opportunity to set up a business with one of his sons as an extension to his existing garden was an opportunity he could not miss and one that I will be eternal grateful for.

Once all the legalities were completed and Dad had handed over what turned out to be a very large cheque, we moved onto the land in late October. Part of the deal was that we were responsible for erecting the fence between our newly purchased plot of land and the main field. Dad saw this as an opportunity to get the land rabbit-proofed, so erecting fencing around the whole site was my first job. Rabbits had always been a problem in Dad's garden and I was determined that they would not be in our new venture.

Having seen the disaster that had befallen Dad when he'd rabbit proofed his own garden, fencing and gates were a priority. He'd done the correct thing and buried his fencing in the ground with the bottom six inches facing into the field next door; that would stop the rabbits that dug down to go under the obstruction in front of them. The problem was that, although he'd erected his fencing quickly, it had taken him about four weeks to get round to putting on the gates. This short gap had allowed the little devils to hop in, and once they were in and settled there was no chance of him getting rid of them.

Having priced the job and got the thumbs-up from the 'bank of Dad' to spend the money, I set about knocking the posts in, digging a trench, erecting the rabbit fencing and getting the rabbit-proof gates in place. My attention then turned to setting up the nursery: the first job here was to erect a shed to house the nursery shop, my office and somewhere to propagate and pot on the plants I would be producing. This would need to be much larger than your average garden shed, so the cost would be greater and I knew that would be problematic having already spent a reasonable amount of Dad's money on fencing.

I'd learned from a young age that the obvious answer was to build our own, but this wasn't something I'd done before: my largest piece of woodwork up to then had been the cabinet I had built while at school! I was sure that once I got started everything would be fine – but how would I start? I had no idea when it came to shed construction. This was not good news and could well have been the end of the new, home-made nursery shed, but fortunately I knew a man who knew a man who could build me one.

It was my friend Tony who came up trumps by suggesting his wife Ali's Uncle Mick, who could apparently build anything from any material put in front of him. He had spent his working life making and repairing articulated lorry trailers so, to me, there was an obvious and easy transition from that to building a shed.

Apparently the only persuasion that he needed was to be told he would be paid, so Mick was tasked with building a 24-foot (7.5m) by 20-foot (6m) building. It would be built in sections in his workshop, with three 8-foot (2.5m) sections per side and two 10-foot (3m) sections for each end. It was a simple enough approach that also worked well with the lengths of wood we could get from the wood merchant to ensure minimal waste.

Once the plans were in place, reality dawned. I was so excited about finding someone to build my shed within Dad's strict budget that I'd forgotten that Mick's workshop was in Kettering, a full twenty-five miles from Barnsdale.

While Mick was busy building the shed panels, I was busy creating the concrete base for the shed to stand on. This would be a solid slab that not only acted as the foundation for the shed but also its floor.

The work was taking place during the winter, always a time of lower income for Dad, so preferably one of minimal spending or no spending at all. To save money, I had an excellent plan for the base that meant we would not need to buy limestone hardcore: the ploughed land we had just purchased was littered with chunks of limestone that had been brought to the surface during the landowner's biannual sub-soiling operation. I soon realised that our heavy clay soil sat on limestone that was bedded in with a proper beige clay, one that could definitely be used to create ceramic masterpieces. I was so pleased with my money-saving idea that I dashed up to pass on this information to Dad. I would collect enough from the stone lying on the ground to fill the bottom of the base. He was delighted that he wouldn't have to spend any more money than was absolutely necessary.

My problem was that I was a bit green when it came to jobs such as this and I hadn't realised how much limestone I needed to establish a good enough base for the concrete to be poured onto. Dad had realised but opted to say nothing.

I spent days bent double with my bucket, which, once filled, was emptied into a wheelbarrow. When that was full, I wheeled it over to the base area and emptied it. For the first two days each barrowful did not seem to make any difference to the area, and by midweek I was beginning to resemble Quasimodo and almost unable to stand up straight. But I was determined not to give in and to see my plan through.

Eventually, after several days of stone collecting, I made it. The limestone had filled the hole I had dug out and reached the base of the shuttering I had erected to contain the fluid concrete. I headed off for a lie down on a nice hard floor to straighten out my back.

The next job was to price up the concrete; as it was a good-sized area, the perfect solution was a lorry full of ready-mixed concrete. I phoned two local companies that provided this service and got a price from each, then took the lowest one to Dad to approve.

I'm sure the first thing he noticed as I strode through

his office door was that I was now back to normal and standing bolt upright, which no doubt influenced what happened next. I explained the volume of concrete I needed, gave him the cheapest quote and waited for his positive response.

Unfortunately, it didn't come. There was a lengthy pause as he considered his options before he announced, with no apparent concession to my still-aching back, that it would be much more economical to mix our own. After all, we had a cement mixer with a petrol engine and the materials we needed could be delivered very close to the base, so there would be minimal exertion.

It was certainly minimal exertion for Dad because he was not going to be doing the mixing, but I knew it was fruitless to even try to counter his argument so I took it on the chin, left his office and went to order the ballast and cement I needed.

I completed the base in super-quick time then borrowed Dad's Land Rover and trailer to make two trips to bring the shed panels from Kettering to Barnsdale. The most important reason for erecting the shed before we did anything else to develop the nursery was because I couldn't get the electricity connected until I had a waterproof place for the main fuse box and meter. My friend Tony, having been instrumental in initiating the shed's construction, returned to the nursery site with me and we unloaded the panels onto the beautifully laid concrete pad.

Once unloaded, Tony helped me continue preparing the site. We even had time to carry out some preparatory work for the perimeter chain-link fence. I really don't know what I would have done without his invaluable help during those initial years, and I tapped his generosity more times than I probably should have done to set up the nursery.

The schedule for shed erection was in place, and this involved Mick coming over to the nursery site the following Saturday to help me and Tony put it up and get it watertight. At eight-thirty on Saturday morning I was ready and waiting for the arrival of my erection team. Tony arrived first; while we waited for Mick, we moved the panels so that they were laying on the ground in the position they would be erected.

Mick arrived just as we finished. I am not so sure about him, but I was very excited at the thought of the nursery taking shape; it might only have been a shed to Mick, but to Dad and me it was the start of our dream.

Immediately Mick arrived we hit a major snag that neither Tony nor I had considered or written into our schedule. We never considered that Mick was 'old school' in his working practices and we were both a bit thrown by his announcement that he could not – and would not – start work until he'd had a cup of tea.

My first reaction was to explain that the main reason for getting the shed erected before doing anything else was so I could get electricity to the nursery, and the only way to boil a kettle was when it was fed by electricity.

All we had at that point was a ploughed field, a concrete pad and several panels of the shed, but Mick was bloody stubborn and stuck rigidly to his guns. Down he sat, his bottom resting firmly on my beautifully prepared concrete base, arms folded, stating that he was not moving until tea had been served!

I had no option but to trek to Dad's workshop to see if he had enough extension leads to plug a kettle into the nearest socket, which was located halfway down his garden, then join one lead to another then another to see if we could get close enough to the concrete pad. Fortunately, Dad turned out to be the extension-lead king and I managed to reach the pad with a lead to spare.

I knew that Dad had already had his morning coffee so I returned to borrow (steal) the kettle as well as grabbing mugs, tea bags and his only bottle of milk. My raid was made much easier because Dad was in the garden and I was sure that I could satisfy Mick's unreasonable demand for a pre-work mug of tea and get everything back in the kitchen before he even realised they'd been 'borrowed'. Dad had no inkling that he'd been robbed, apart from the fact that he now had less milk in his bottle and three dirty mugs in his otherwise empty sink!

Mick was full of tea and the panels had been well made, so erecting the shed went ahead without any real problem. Mick was on his way back home before lunchtime leaving Tony and me to put the roof trusses in place and attach the roofing boards before attaching the felt to them.

Although an electrician by trade, my amazing friend Tony can turn his hand to anything. Just before nightfall the shed was waterproof and ready to be connected to the National Grid, and I booked a date for him to come back and fit the lights and sockets. Within two weeks I was blessed with a large shed (with electricity) and a couple of beds ready for the saleable plants I had been producing.

Being keen on plants, and even more keen on propagating them, I knew that I'd have no problem filling however many sales beds I erected, but an empty space like the shed always seems larger than it really is when you're standing in the middle of it. Once I'd erected a potting bench, sales counter and a small, enclosed space in the corner for an office, I wondered if I actually had enough space – though I would never have dared tell Dad I thought my shed might be too small!

Sales began well, with people keen to buy the more unusual plants I was growing and selling, but progress in developing the remainder of the nursery was often slow, not because of a lack of effort on my part but because of the noise my hard work was making. Every Friday when the BBC came to film, Dad reminded me not to make any noise so I spent all my time trying to do as much as I could as quietly as I could.

It never ceased to amaze me how sensitive the BBC

microphones were. My phone would often ring with Dad asking if I was making the loud noises when most of the time I thought I was making no noise at all! It got to the point where even silence seemed to generate a phone call and I felt I would have to stop breathing for fear that the microphones would pick up that sound, too. It was funny how, purely by chance, it seemed that the nursery jobs creating intolerable noise for a BBC sound man always seemed to take place on a Friday.

I was not the only noise problem when they were filming; John Kenyon's earlier persuasive performance came back to haunt Dad and the film crew. Having persuaded the RAF to move the Tornado's flight path from over Barnsdale, a couple of years later Dad had to move a mile up the road – right under the new flight path! Although John tried at least twice to persuade the RAF to move the flight path again, he only managed to confuse them. As far as the station commander was concerned he had *already* moved the flight path so he must have concluded that they were dealing with a mad man.

The planes stayed on the same path every time they flew over, so Dad was forced to take action particularly when he was rattling off a very long piece to camera. When I say 'a long piece', this was usually a continuous recording of around two minutes either talking straight to camera or while talking and carrying out a particular task in the garden. There were times when he was well-past halfway and he heard the sound of a Tornado jet in the distance. That prompted him to speed up to try and beat the jet to the end of his piece. Sometimes he won and sometimes he didn't, but if you watch his performances carefully you can certainly spot when he beat the Tornado: it was just a pity that nobody recorded his beaming smile and obvious pride when he turned out to be the winner!

Chapter Ten

It was whilst developing the nursery from scratch it became clear that my creative and inventive craftiness was almost identical to Dad's. I'd had an inkling about that previously, but it seemed that the innovative ways I used to persuade him to part with the money were all down to the 'Hamilton crafty genes' I had inherited.

It was amazing how similar the techniques I used on Dad were to those he used to extract money from the BBC. Getting *any* money from them was not an easy task; the Corporation deemed *Gardeners' World* one of their star programmes and didn't feel that it needed investment. To squeeze even a tiny amount out of their purse he had to be inventive in his approach.

Such an occasion happened when he moved from the original Barnsdale to the site we occupy now. Everyone in the film crew knew that Dad was moving to a house with a field so he would be starting from scratch. He had just purchased a small farmhouse, which came with five and a half acres of land, four of which he could turn into a garden space. Conveniently, these were not all down to pasture but bordered on the eastern boundary by a bank of predominantly mature beech trees. He also owned this stretch of trees which, in their entirety, formed the mile-long avenue of trees growing on each side of The Avenue.

The trees were more than fifty feet (15m) high, and he knew that he needed to use not just this fantastic naturally created height he had inherited, but also the amazing views of rural Rutland over his western boundary hedge. Bringing in views of crops, fields, hedgerows and trees to the west so that they became part of his garden wouldn't be difficult, but how best to use the trees?

Once his brain clicked into gear he had a great idea – but how to pitch it to John? Rather than jump straight in, he let the idea rattle around in his head for a few days before a plan of action started to take shape.

Dad knew that the optimum time to pitch his idea was during their lunch break in the kitchen. Once settled with a selection of cheeses on a platter next to a large, fresh, white loaf, Dad casually mentioned a new horticultural technique. Taking another mouthful of bread and cheese, he waited for this innovation to sink in before emphasising that it should be something that would be of REAL interest to the viewers of *Gardeners' World*. John was not so sure.

Later that day Dad discovered that John's reservations about this cutting-edge technique related to the cost of having it as a feature on *Gardeners' World* and introducing this new-fangled thing to the public. As John dug in his heels over the potential cost, Dad knew that he'd need to pull a masterstroke to change his mind. He needed a trump card and, fortunately for the UK gardening public, that was just what he had up his sleeve.

There was nothing else for it but to lay all his cards – including the trump card – on the table. He announced, 'If we feature this on *Gardeners' World*, it will be a television first,' and smiled as he finished. The smile was not just to encourage John to agree but also because he was so proud of his trump card.

He had pitched it perfectly. His statement was like a red rag to a bull and an invitation that John could not allow to pass him by. He left Barnsdale, having promised Dad that he would take the written proposal to 'the BBC man who held the purse strings' and would be as persuasive as possible. (This was the only title Dad ever heard the BBC money man mentioned by and never actually knew his name.)

Dad waited anxiously until, a couple of days later, he got the phone call from John with the positive message that he had secured the money for the project.

The feature he was adamant they needed to put in front of the nation's avid gardeners was indeed new and involved some heavy machinery in order to dig up semi-mature and mature trees. These were much bigger than those that tree growers had previously been able to raise and sell, and they needed to be dug up with as much of the roots left intact as possible.

The machine had big spade-like attachments driven

by hydraulics, which meant that they could dig around a large tree, grab the large root ball and lift it out of the hole in one seamless movement. Once the tree was out of the ground the machine, on caterpillar tracks, could move it to a waiting vehicle or to an already prepared hole for replanting.

The ability to lift trees of this size was revolutionary for the horticultural industry and absolutely perfect for those who needed more mature specimens. It was also suitable for people who didn't have the patience to wait for a smaller tree to grow in their own garden – but it came at a cost.

This technique was a real find and a result of Dad's continuous search for new projects to show viewers of *Gardeners' World* but – and it is a very big but – he also had an ulterior motive. He knew where there were some semi-mature trees that he needed to move close to the bank of trees on his eastern boundary, thus creating the link he needed to start elevating his otherwise flat land.

This was an opportunity not to be missed and everything seemed to be falling into place. His first thought was definitely to benefit his viewers by demonstrating the tree-lifting technique, but between mentioning his idea to John and waiting for the go-ahead he realised that he could kill two birds with one stone. For John, since the money had been allocated and the services of the company offering this new technique had been secured for an unbelievably low cost, his biggest worry was where they were going to find some trees to move.

I can only assume that John was still on a high because he didn't seem to notice the blindingly obvious. After excitedly telling Dad how little he'd had to spend he asked the question that had been troubling him. 'We have the giant spade machine coming in two weeks, but no established trees to use to demonstrate the technique.'

John knew that the bank of trees on the east side of Dad's garden were too large, but he didn't seem to notice when Dad's response was so rapid that it must have been premeditated.

'It's funny you should say that,' was Dad's opening line. 'Before I moved from the original Barnsdale, I asked the owners if I could take three trees from the garden area around the cottage. They are the perfect size for this demonstration.'

Amazingly, John seemed to believe what he'd been told without being aware of the planning behind it; even more amazingly, Dad contained his excitement when John agreed this was just what they needed. It seemed he was just happy that at least they could use the machinery the BBC had just paid for!

Dad wanted to move silver birch as these were the first trees he'd planted when he'd moved into the cottage five years earlier. The day came for the big move and everything went according to plan with the tree lifting, the move up the road and the replanting in an area that would become Dad's woodland.

John conceded that Dad had come up with an excellent idea, was impressed with the piece they'd filmed for *Gardeners' World* and knew that his bosses would be over the moon with the impact versus the cost. Dad was delighted that he'd managed to get his three large trees moved and planted to link his tall beech trees with his garden space without him spending a penny of his own money!

The whole tree-moving event made a spectacular insert into that particular *Gardeners' World* programme. Better still, John never discovered Dad's cunning plan. Dad certainly slept well knowing that he had educated millions of *Gardeners' World* viewers in a new, cutting-edge horticultural technique and was also now the proud owner of three newly planted large trees.

Dad encountered numerous unusual events while working for the BBC, mostly concerning money or the lack of it but some more personal. The issues around money greatly annoyed him because they held him back and prevented the team from taking *Gardeners' World* to an even higher level by creating even more benefits for their viewers. These money issues were a constant theme the whole time he was presenting the programme.

It was even more galling when money was wasted, no more so than when they asked two prominent garden designers, Robin Williams and John Brookes, to design two different herb gardens for a small feature on the programme. Robin Williams designed a romantic area that was meant to be a small part of a larger garden, while John Brookes designed a more symmetrical and modern one. Whoever ordered the materials for Robin's garden managed to order twice as much as he needed, so once Dad had finished building the feature he still had the same amount left as he'd used. When he informed the BBC, he was told that sending the excess back was too expensive!

To a keen recycler, this was an opportunity not to be missed. I was summoned to his office and then out to the front of the house where the leftover material was piled up. As we stared at the bricks, sand, cement, brick paviours and wood, Dad announced that I could have it all and recreate Robin's romantic herb garden in the nursery garden area. That was music to my ears because, like Dad, I couldn't turn down the offer of something for free – and I certainly wasn't turning down the offer of having a Robin Williams' designed garden space for free!

What infuriated Dad even more was when, at the end of the series, he was told by a BBC employee that if he wanted to keep both the Robin Williams' and John Brookes' herb features in his garden, he would have to stump up the cost of the materials. When he told me I stood open-mouthed, unable to conjure any words that might make that statement sound even partly reasonable.

This was not something Dad was prepared to do, so both gardens were taken up and the materials sent back to where the BBC had told him they needed to go. He informed the Corporation, but somehow forgot to mention that they'd sent twice the amount and that he'd kept the excess! Nobody from the BBC ever mentioned the excess, so we carried on as if it had never happened. My Robin Williams' herb area was safe and, more than thirty years later, it is still here and still giving as much pleasure and education to visitors as it did all those years ago when it was first broadcast.

The gazebo in the Paradise Town Garden was the total opposite because it was Dad who managed to overspend. By the time he came to write and prepare both the gardens for the *Paradise Gardens* series so that they were ready for the first day of shooting, he'd been presenting on *Gardeners' World* for fifteen years. However, it had taken him less than fifteen weeks from his first day of working with the BBC in 1979 to realise that every job came with a budget that was non-negotiable upwards – although the Corporation was always very pleased if he came in under budget!

Once the *Paradise Gardens* series had been written and designed, the next stage was to cost everything required for the two gardens he was going to build. As Dad was accustomed to doing with these short series, he would build a cheaper garden then a totally different and more expensive one because the garden that cost less to create balanced out the extravagance of the other one, much to the pleasure of the BBC. Once priced up, the information was sent to the BBC and included within the overall budget for this series of six programmes.

The Paradise Town Garden was the more expensive of the two and had been created to give viewers an idea of what was possible within an enclosed space. The main problem was that we did not have an enclosed space to develop so we needed to create one, ideally surrounded by a wall.

Dad had a walled garden built and installed a pond in it, which was made more formal by the addition of a lion's head fountain set against the opposite wall. The recycled water from the pond came out of the lion's mouth into a rill that ran back into the pond. He installed a patio that was ideal as a seating area for relaxing where your eyes would be drawn across the pond, up the rill to the lion's head fountain. As this would be a place to relax, he wanted to have the seat covered so it could be used whatever the weather and the ideal structure for this was a gazebo. Not any old gazebo, of course; this one needed to look stunning and would therefore have to be bespoke.

Fortunately for him and the millions who watched this series, his good friend Peter Wallace happened to be a craftsman with wood, so Dad tasked him with designing and creating this magnificent gazebo. Peter's design and quote were both accepted, not just by Dad but also by BBC producer Ray Hough, and Peter set about building. What a splendid construction he produced!

Once it was finished, he came to Barnsdale, positioned

it and attached the cedar shingles to the Chinese-inspired roof. Dad gazed in admiration, not only of Peter's craftsmanship but also how the gazebo complemented the garden. He congratulated Peter on how well he'd interpreted Dad's original concept – but he couldn't get a tiny nagging thought out of his head. Much as he loved it (and I knew he loved it because he often tootled down from his office to have an admiring gaze at it before tootling back again), he felt there was something missing and to him this gave the impression of it being unfinished.

Peter came back to Barnsdale to talk the problem through. As they stood there looking at it, he understood Dad's view and suggested that he should chat with a friend who was a local woodcarver. He was sure this woodcarver could create whatever Dad needed to 'finish off' the gazebo. Peter's suggestion was to have six carvings placed in the six triangle spaces he'd created between each supporting leg and the base of the roof, and apparently the perfect man for the job was Glyn Mould.

Glyn came to Barnsdale to see if Dad's initial ideas were workable and, most importantly, achievable. The end result was six stunning triangular wildlife carvings: a spider and web; a hedgehog; a bee on a flower; a bird in a bush; a frog, and a bird on a branch. Once they were installed, they elevated the already spectacular gazebo to something even Dad could never have envisaged.

As with virtually all great things, there is often a

negative side, sometimes huge and sometimes miniscule, and this structure was no exception. The carvings were an after-thought, so they were not part of the original calculations and therefore not part of the final budget. Don't forget that this budget had been 'set in stone'.

As far as Dad was concerned, the crux of the problem was that the cost of these carvings now had to be added to the budget. To get the *Paradise Gardens* project past the holder of the BBC purse strings, he had trimmed the costs to the bone so there was no room for manoeuvre to balance the budget. He knew he had to do something, but he had no idea how to broach the subject of the carvings to Ray Hough because they'd cost as much as the gazebo!

Eventually, after much cogitating, he decided that the best way to get the BBC to pay for them was to say nothing and act as if they'd always been part of the plan and therefore part of the budget. He had formed a great relationship with Ray Hough and knew that this would not be affected by the carvings' episode because money was dealt with by a different BBC department.

He placed the invoice for the carvings in the middle of a pile of other invoices for goods spent on items for the series in the faint hope that it would automatically go through the payment process and nobody would be any the wiser.

Unbelievably, a couple of weeks later Dad received a phone call from Glyn to thank him for the cheque he'd received in the post that morning from the BBC!

Dad put down the receiver with a huge sigh of relief; he felt that was proof that he'd got away with his crafty overspend.

In all his years on *Gardeners' World*, Dad became known for his budgeting ideas and this was undoubtedly the best way to get something in the cheapest way possible: getting someone else to pay for it! In Dad's defence, the carvings really did pay for themselves as a visual feature throughout the *Paradise Gardens* series and have been delighting visitors to the gardens ever since.

Dad was so impressed with Glyn's carvings that he got thoroughly carried away and asked him to carve a front door to replace the boring wooden one that had been there since he'd moved in thirteen years earlier; he wanted a door that was all about Barnsdale. Glyn wasn't going to turn down such a commission and it only took him a couple of weeks to return with a sketch of his ideas for the four carved panels of the door. Dad agreed that the design was perfect and gave him the go-ahead to start carving.

To produce such intricate images on a door was not going to be cheap, so Dad saw no reason to hold back on the quality of the wood and asked Glyn to make it from English oak. One of his favourite sayings was 'if a job is worth doing then it is worth doing well' and this job, when finished would last so long that it would see him out, plus his children, grandchildren and his great-grandchildren!

Glyn must have worked day and night on the door because he turned up to fit it much sooner than anyone expected. When he removed it from his van it was covered in protective dust sheets and when the unveiling took place, I swear I saw a small tear in the corner of Dad's eye. It is very hard to explain the quality of this door, short of saying that it was truly the work of a master craftsman. It was Dad's pride and joy – which meant that I had definitely slipped down the rankings!

I am sure that he began popping out for things he didn't really need just so he could return home, admire his new front door and then pass through it.

Unfortunately, not all of Glyn's masterful work had a positive effect on those who saw it.

The door, once installed, was fantastic and so much more than Dad had hoped. When he looked closely at each of the four carved panels, he could see that the quality he'd seen in the carvings for his *Paradise Town* garden gazebo had been replicated. However, the problem with such magnificence is that it needs to be inspected both at close quarters and from a distance to get the full benefit, as I discovered years later during a guided walk.

Occasionally I am asked to give a paid-for guided walk around the gardens, usually for coach groups. These tours generally last around two hours and we look at most of the individual gardens, then the group members are free to go back and look more closely at the ones they liked or we haven't been able to see.

On a sunny July day in 2012, I was with a group of thirty or so keen gardeners. They had all managed to keep up with me as I led them round the gardens, listened to what I'd said and even asked the odd question. In what seemed no time at all, we made it virtually all the way around and there were only four more gardens to look at. Then disaster struck.

I was totally unprepared for what was about to happen. We were in the *Paradise Town* garden and I had explained to my lovely group the reasons behind the design and layout, then talked about the gazebo and explained why it was positioned where it was. The group members were standing on the entrance path to the garden, the patio in front of the conservatory and the path between the back border and the pond.

Once I'd finished talking about the pond, rill and lion's head fountain, I continued somewhat excitably to talk about Peter Wallace and his gazebo, and Glyn Mould and the carvings. I tend not to stay in this garden too long because I'm aware that we have been walking for around an hour and forty-five minutes so the sound of running water could send most of my group rushing towards the facilities!

Before we left, I mentioned that on their return visit to this particular garden they needed to get close to the carvings then to step back and look at the gazebo as a whole. This was an excellent piece of advice and one I hoped they would all heed.

They nodded – but as I turned to leave the garden I

heard an almighty splash followed by a collective gasp. I turned back just as a head burst through the surface of the pond water, rapidly followed by the top half of a lady from my group. She was spluttering, covered in pond weed, and had such a look of shock on her face – which rapidly turned to embarrassment when she realised that it was not just me staring down at her but also the rest of her group. A few of us helped her to get out of this watery predicament, whilst her husband seemed to disappear to the back, probably in an attempt to disassociate himself from the whole affair.

Once she was free of the pond and safely back on terra firma, I asked the obvious question, 'Are you alright?'

She sounded subdued as she said, 'Yes, I'm fine thanks. I only stepped back to take a better look.' This was close to the advice I'd just given – but stepping back without looking behind you is never a good idea.

I already knew the answer to the next question but I felt compelled to ask as it had all gone very quiet and I felt that someone needed to say something. 'Do you have a spare set of clothes with you?' I asked.

As expected, 'no' was the short reply. By this time my brain was working overtime to find a way out of this pickle. I remembered that I had a large towel in my office (I have no idea why), so I asked her to come with me and left the group in the capable hands of Jon, my head gardener. He finished the tour while we went towards the nursery shop.

Steam must have been coming out of my ears as my

brain worked at supersonic speed until I came up with the perfect solution. I explained that we had a disabled toilet where she could undress, dry herself, then wrap herself in the towel whilst I dashed up to the shed and popped her wet clothes in the washing machine for a spin before transferring them to our tumble dryer.

Once she'd got over the fact that I'd just told her to get undressed, she agreed that this was an excellent idea and waited in the disabled toilet until the dryer cycle had finished.

After an hour her clothes were dry enough for her to dress and leave the disabled toilet, which was fortunate because her group were sitting down for lunch. She joined them and sat next to her husband, who had finally re-emerged. After about ten minutes, they moved from the bothy room to an outside table; that may have seemed odd to the others in their group, but I understood: having retrieved her clothes from the tumble dryer, I knew that the smell of pond embedded in them was quite overwhelming!

I didn't see the coach leave at the end of their visit, so I have no idea if the majority of passengers voted to place her in the luggage compartment! I think this lady will think twice before taking a step backwards to get a better look; the event also enlightened me because previously I'd only thought about how to prevent children from falling into any of our ponds!

□□□

If the BBC hadn't taken up the forerunner of *Geoff Hamilton's Paradise Gardens*, this spectacular series would not have been made and knowledge-hungry viewers would have been deprived of two superb gardening productions.

The first of the three short series Dad wrote and presented was *The Ornamental Kitchen Garden*, which consisted of a garden that he'd built and planted the year before filming with the idea of using it when everything was finished and established. Over the six programmes, he rebuilt the garden to show people how it had been done, cutting each time between the original and the finished product.

His concept was to create an ornamental garden that could be productive; he was adamant that it would not be a productive garden with a few ornamentals planted in it just to perk it up. Dad always worked at his best with people who understood his vision and Mark Kershaw, the producer of this series, was the perfect fit. They got on like a house on fire and Mark also used cutting-edge television techniques. Together they created not just a wonderful series but a garden that continues to inspire those who come and see it more than thirty-five years later.

When the garden was finished it was amazing. You had to look hard to see the vegetables and, of course, seed catalogues in the late 1980s didn't carry the wide range of ornamental vegetable varieties that they do today.

It was a real masterstroke, with Dad often having to point out the vegetables to the crew. The garden was not just about vegetables and ornamentals, though, it was also about fruit. He'd planted fan-trained fruit trees, step-over apples, a fig, a peach and even trained an apple tree into a lollipop shape for those who only had the tiniest of gardens and wanted a fruiting apple tree.

The Ornamental Kitchen Garden was a great success, with the viewing figure exceeding all expectations, but when he approached the BBC three years later with his next series they were not so keen and told him that it was not something they wanted to film at that time.

There was never any question that Dad was a man of great foresight and he'd been presenting for long enough to know when something would be a success. His main problem was that he was dealing with a BBC executive who probably had no interest in gardening and who couldn't see the great potential that Dad saw. Mind you, it was this type of pin-striped suit wearers that sent David Bowie away, telling him that he was talentless and had no future as a pop star. Although Dad could sing, he was in no way comparable to Bowie as a pop star – but could David garden as well as Dad did? Highly unlikely!

Dad was not a quitter so a few weeks later he tried again but came away with the same rebuff. He knew that it was an absolute certainty that his concept would be a success, but how to persuade the BBC executives?

He decided that he would go for broke. After

persuading them to allow him one more meeting, he announced that if they were not interested he would have no option but to offer his idea to Channel 4. That comment certainly perked up their ears and – surprise, surprise – suddenly they wanted to hear more. In a flash they were keen to see a draft of the first episode and a precis of the other five.

Leaving the meeting full of the joys of spring, Dad dashed home and started pummelling his computer keys until he'd rattled off a version of the first episode that he was pleased with, followed by an outline of the other five episodes. He sealed the printed sheets in an envelope and sent it to the BBC. Before he even had time to start thinking about what would go into the draft of the second episode, a call came through saying that they would be more than happy to proceed as long as the budget allowed. It seemed as if the BBC executives had taken the Channel 4 threat very seriously indeed.

Fortunately for Dad, he'd planned to expand what he had done with his first series and build two different gardens to show his viewers contrasting ideas. Although they would both be similar in size, one would be built for someone with above-average income, whilst the other was not only very cheap and aimed at the average gardener but would be built within the boundary of the second ornamental kitchen garden so he didn't need to buy fencing. The ideas were all there and he was pretty sure that the whole series would come in under budget, so he was up and running.

The budget was approved, Dad was given the thumbs up and a producer, Andrew Gosling, was allocated to the project. Before going any further, Dad knew that he needed to meet with this producer of what was to become *Geoff Hamilton's Cottage Gardens*.

He was very lucky because he and Andrew quickly fell into an excellent working relationship; Dad knew that Andrew was the final piece of the jigsaw that would see his vison become reality. The filming seemed to go without a hitch and Dad had such an enjoyable time creating his two gardens at Barnsdale, as well as going out and about to be filmed talking to other cottage gardeners in their own gardens. But, much as he loved presenting and meeting other like-minded gardeners, it was the creating that gave him the most pleasure, from the initial designs through to the building and the planting.

The artisan's cottage garden was the cheaper of the two and aimed at the gardener who had little to spend whose focus was on the plants they loved. Most of the plants he used were self-propagated using seed, cuttings or division, which made them very cheap. There were some bought plants such as the trained fruit, but these were kept to an absolute minimum to keep down the cost. There were four rectangular beds in the centre of the garden and narrow ones along the fence line, all of which were edged with rough-sawn wood, while the pathways were covered with a thin layer of pea shingle.

If the artisan's garden was cheap and cheerful, the gentleman's cottage garden was the complete opposite. It cost much more and was aimed at the minority of cottage gardeners who had plenty of money to spend. This garden was formal, whilst the artisan's was wilder and woollier.

It was surrounded by what would become a beautifully clipped, yew hedge. The pathways were made from hand-made York bricks, which look old the minute they are laid, while the trellis and arches were made from hardwood. Obviously there was a cost implication to this, but when Andrew Gosling asked if the cost of the trellis and arches was justified Dad said that not only did their quality better suit this garden than their cheaper softwood cousins, but they would last for several generations.

He felt that this explanation was sufficient but Andrew had a reply: 'But Geoff, we're not going to be here for several generations.' Dad had no come back to this excellent response but still managed to get his way!

The two gardens were such a contrast in style (as well as cost) that they covered everything Dad and Andrew hoped for. Many viewers who could not afford the expense of the gentleman's cottage garden still gleaned ideas from it that they could adapt to fit their own gardens.

Throughout filming Dad felt that things were falling into place and the series could not get any better – but this belief was not only about to be tested but blown out of the water.

He discovered George Flatt and, just like all the best things in life, he came across him completely by chance. A researcher who was looking for suitable cottage gardens and gardeners to feature in the series gave him the details of a lady with a garden in deepest Norfolk that would be perfect for the series.

When he arrived, Dad quickly realised that this was not the type of garden he wanted to feature in the series, so he used the offer of tea and cake as the opportunity to let the owner down gently by explaining why. He had just got to the crucial point of the 'why' when she burst out, 'Oh well, if it's that sort of garden and person you're looking for, you should meet my Uncle George.'

Fortunately Uncle George only lived a short distance away, so Dad thought he could examine his garden quickly and be on his way home after what seemed to be a wasted journey.

I'm not sure you can eat your thoughts as you can your words, but this was about to be Dad's fate! George Flatt lived in the cottage where he'd been born, as most of his ancestors had done, and his niece said he was not just a gardener but a character, too.

Dad said his goodbyes and staggered to his car, stomach full of Victoria sponge, to find Uncle George. George must have been forewarned because when Dad arrived at his thatched cottage he was standing by the old wooden gate, leaning on his hoe and waiting for his visitor.

They shook hands and Dad was blown away by the sheer joy that was this man. He could have stayed in the garden listening to George for several weeks, and he came away knowing that he had found the star of his series.

Dad was more than happy to tell people that the series would have been nowhere near as good without George Flatt, who was unquestionably the very thick layer of icing on a delicious cake, but although he was over the moon with how well the finished version came together, he knew that now it was finished it was crunch time.

Knowing how much importance the BBC placed on viewing figures, if Dad wanted to make another series this one had to get close to the 4.5 million viewers *Gardeners' World* was attracting each week. What made him more anxious was that he already had a seed of an idea for a follow-up series; he also knew that reaching the weekly average viewing numbers of *Gardeners' World* was a big ask because his *Cottage Garden* series would be broadcast during the winter months when many people had stopped gardening.

We all have those moments in life when we wonder what an earth we were doing spending so much time worrying about something that turned out not to be problematic at all. Well, this was one of those moments for Dad because not long after the sixth and final episode was broadcast, the viewing figures were published and *Geoff Hamilton's Cottage Gardens* series averaged more than nine million viewers per programme!

It was a phenomenon, one which the BBC was not expecting and something they had not experienced from a gardening programme before. And to think they'd nearly lost it to Channel 4!

This time they were quick to act. Only a week after the final programme and hours after the viewing figures were published, Dad got a phone call from a BBC executive who was quite obviously buttering him up. The executive told him how happy they were with the series, what a great success it had been and what a great writer and presenter Dad was before moving onto the real reason he'd phoned.

Much to Dad's disbelief, he was told that a second series was always something the BBC had considered, this was something they definitely wanted and they wanted it **NOW**!

He was somewhat miffed that the BBC had conveniently forgotten that they'd initially turned down this series twice, but his annoyance dissipated when he realised that *Geoff Hamilton's Paradise Gardens* was about to be born. He knew how well the formula of building two gardens worked, so his next series would also consist of one cheaper and one more expensive garden, with both being built at Barnsdale.

His initial idea was to create a garden with a woodland glade feel to it and the other to be in an enclosed space. These would give viewers ideas about how to create their own little piece of paradise whether that was in their back garden, their front garden or even their allotment. He decided that the enclosed space would be the more expensive of the two so it would have to be a formal and walled garden, while the woodland glade would not only cheaper but also have a more natural feel.

He had the vision but nothing on paper, although this did not seem to deter the BBC in their determination to film the series and have it ready to go in ten months. They did not realise that this was unachievable until Dad explained that he needed time to write, research other gardens and gardeners to visit and build the two gardens at Barnsdale, while also needing time for the plants to grow.

He was absolutely stunned by the BBC employee's response: 'Oh, do the plants have to grow?' After all the years he'd worked with non-gardening members of BBC staff Dad should have known better; he certainly knew now what he was working with and battling against!

A date was agreed to start filming. Dad had decided that he would stick with his original idea for the two gardens at Barnsdale, so naming them Town Paradise Garden and Country Paradise Garden, he began to write.

He got to the end of part five of the six programmes, and with the filming date fast approaching, decided to see what I thought of what he'd written so far. He tootled down to find me potting in my nursery shed, pinned me in a corner and gave me a summary of what was already down on paper, as well as the basic ideas for the programmes to come.

My response was positive with one massive exception: the walled Town Paradise Garden. I thought it was an excellent idea and the planting inside it was spot on, but I had reservations about the surrounding wall. More than once I'd had to deal with the planning department at Rutland County Council and I knew how long the process took. I explained that the first thing he needed to do was not to write the series but to apply for planning permission for the wall.

Presumably because I had pointed out the need for the planning permission, applying for it was passed onto me. Knowing how soon they wanted to start filming it would be problematic getting it in time, so before I filled in the paperwork I phoned the planning department of Rutland County Council to find out the best approach.

Having explained our predicament to a very helpful planning officer, I was told we had no chance of getting the planning application through before filming was due to start, let alone getting the wall built in time. He suggested that the best thing would be to build the wall and apply for retrospective planning permission. He finished by telling me that, although he could not guarantee the outcome, he was 99.9% sure that the council would not turn down our application for, what in effect was, a garden wall.

Buoyed by this information, my next job was to find a builder because, unsurprisingly, somehow that had also become my responsibility.

The search for a builder took no time at all because I went straight to the person who knew everyone: my friend Tony. Yet again he had the answer: the son-in-law of my shed builder Mick worked for a builder who apparently had an excellent reputation.

When I met the builder on site at Barnsdale, he told me more than once that he was not just a good builder, he had been awarded 'The Golden Trowel'! Once he'd finished talking himself up, I explained exactly what we wanted and the timescale, and asked him to send his quote in double-quick time.

When it arrived I took it to Dad; it seemed very reasonable and the builder had confirmed that he could complete the work by the deadline. Dad and I were both reassured by the thought of 'The Golden Trowel' so we agreed to proceed.

Then Dad dropped his bombshell. Bearing in mind how hard I'd been working to make sure everything required could be completed before the first day of filming, he suddenly announced that I should agree the quote with the builder but no work would begin until Dad got the first instalment of money from the BBC to pay for it. He was adamant that there was still a chance that the series could be pulled, and he didn't want to spend that sort of money on something that might not happen.

Fortunately the cheque arrived within a few days, so Mr Golden Trowel arrived to start work. As the foundations were being laid, I filled in the planning application and delivered the forms to the council offices. The construction would consist of a back wall of approximately 4m (13ft) (which would mimic a house wall), the two side walls were 1.8m (6ft) and the front wall would be 1.2m (4ft). It was important to have the front wall lower so the cameraman could film into the garden without constantly running up and down a ladder. The rear 'house wall' had a doorway in the centre and the front wall had a gateway slightly off-centre.

The walls seemed to rise very quickly, but it was only after the mortar had dried in the tall, rear one that we noticed its different shades. A professional builder should ensure that every mortar mix has exactly the same quantities of each component, thus making the mixes exactly the same colour. The problem with the different shades was that it gave a patchwork effect, not the look Dad was hoping for or expecting. I think my contribution to the discussion on how this had happened helped him feel better when I suggested that maybe some of the gold from the builder's 'Golden Trowel' had leaked into the mix!

In the end it turned out not to be too problematic or noticeable when filmed because Dad had a conservatory in his design that would be placed on the wall and hide almost all the variation; the rest was hidden by the climbing plants he subsequently grew.

The erroneous mortar was hidden in a very horticultural way but the brick-laying problems were not quite over. When the conservatory team arrived to install it, they found that the brick wall base was not appropriate. Mr Golden Trowel had been given the exact measurements, an accurately drawn plan and been told that the wall had to meet these very precise stipulations or the conservatory would not fit onto the low wall base – but he still managed to end up with a wall that was not remotely close to what it should have been. The only option was to knock it down and rebuild it – but this time Dad insisted on a local builder without a precious-metal trowel!

Although Dad paid Mr Golden Trowel, he refused to pay for the conservatory wall part of the job. The only reason he didn't reduce the amount for the other walls was because he didn't get charged for the aborted installation visit by the conservatory people; they were just delighted that their product would appear in front of millions of prime-time BBC viewers.

Dad's plan was to fill the conservatory with tender plants to cover the back wall and to give it interest for twelve months of the year. In order to do that, he had heating installed. The conservatory was painted a lovely dark-green colour and Dad even managed to blag some paint in order to make the gazebo the same colour and tie them together.

◻◻◻

I'm not sure if Dad manufactured opportunities to implement his natural craftiness or it was something that just happened at the time. It was not just with the BBC that he implemented this talent; he used it many times in his everyday life.

A prime example was with local farmer, Ken Williamson. Ken rented a farmhouse, stables and about forty acres of land from the local landowner, and his farm was only half a mile along the Cottesmore Road from Barnsdale. Dad had not met Ken, but one evening he found himself in a deserted Noel Arms when a man strode in looking for something to quench his thirst after a long day sitting on a tractor.

For Dad it was one of those moments when you think you know someone but there's the nagging doubt that they might resemble someone you know and you don't actually know them at all. This was definitely one of those moments.

As Ken approached the bar he nodded in Dad's direction as he was the only other person there, then leant against the bar and ordered his well-deserved pint of Ruddles County Ale. He watched the barman pour it into a pint glass, seeming to long for the moment he could open his mouth and gulp it down. By the time it arrived, he had quite obviously worked himself into such a Ruddles' frenzy that he drank half of it in a matter of seconds.

Dad was interested to know what the urgency was, so he asked and that started a conversation that continued until closing time. Dad was in no rush, though unfortunately Ken had told his wife he was only popping out for a swift pint!

Dad was embarrassed when he discovered that Ken was a neighbour because Ken knew all about Dad and Barnsdale but Dad knew nothing about Ken and Jenny Williamson, even though he'd passed their rented farmhouse many times on his frequent trips to the village stores in Cottesmore.

This ignorance on Dad's part was about to work in his favour. The conversation turned to Ken's farm and Dad discovered it was rented from the local landowner. He mentioned the dealings he'd had with them when he'd bought Barnsdale and the land for the nursery, but Ken was keener to focus on the amount of rent he was paying for his farm.

His next topic was the cost of farm machinery before he moved onto the stables on the farm and the problems they caused him because his wife used them as livery for horses.

Dad supped his pint of beer slowly as he waited for an opportunity to say something – he wasn't sure what, but he would think of something to contribute! He prepared to change the subject to something a bit more positive but sensed that the direction in which Ken seemed to be heading could be favourable.

Ken wasn't moaning about the horses or his wife but that everything Jenny fed them in one end seemed to come out in greater volume at the other end. He'd got to the point where he was struggling to cope with the piles of manure. He was already using all he needed, but still it piled up. He was at a loss as how to prevent his farm being buried under a mound of horse manure.

Fortunately for Ken, he was sitting beside the man who could solve his problem. From the machinery conversation, Dad knew that Ken had a tractor with a front-end loader bucket and a couple of trailers. A plan began to take shape in his head.

'How much manure are you looking to get rid of, Ken?' was his opening salvo. He had already heard most of Ken's life history and his problems by then, so felt comfortable using first names.

'To be honest, Geoff, I could do with getting rid of at least half of the muck we have piled in the field,' came the reply.

Dad looked pensive, took another swig of his beer and rehearsed his plan before speaking to make sure he didn't slip up.

Ken was rightly under the impression that Dad was thinking of ways to get rid of the muck – which he was – but not in the way the farmer anticipated.

After a long pause, Dad said, 'If you're really desperate, Ken, I can help you out and take some of the muck off your hands.' A smile started to appear on Ken's face, at which point Dad saw the opportunity to deliver his killer line: 'I think I can take virtually all of it but the problem is that I don't have anything to transport it in.'

He had Ken exactly where he wanted him and spent the last part of the evening persuading him that it would be beneficial for both parties if Ken delivered the manure. By the end of the evening, Ken had agreed to bring Dad as many trailer loads of well-rotted horse manure as he needed.

The first load was delivered by Ken's son, Anthony, and was to be filmed for *Gardeners' World*. He arrived at the allotted time with a large trailer full to the brim. He backed up to the desired spot and the camera started to roll as the trailer lifted and its contents slid out into a very neat pile on the ground. Both Dad and Anthony were then stunned to hear the producer announce that they would just shoot that again but from a different angle. I think the reply was something like, 'Well, only if you're prepared to shovel it all back in!'

Each year from then on, Ken delivered six large trailer-loads of manure and tipped each of them wherever Dad needed them – and until the day he retired he always felt grateful to Dad for helping him out.

It had all been a bit a fun for Dad in the pub and he had every intention of telling Ken so, but this agreement turned out to be a symbiotic relationship and he became a good friend of the Williamsons. He was aware that he needed to wait until Ken's gratitude for his Good Samaritan deed waned before he told him the truth so Ken didn't feel he'd been taken advantage of. That day never came but it didn't really matter. Every time I saw Ken, he always told me how grateful he'd been for the horse-manure disposal service Dad had given him!

Chapter Eleven

Although the manure from Ken was not 100% organic because the horses had been inoculated when necessary, this was the route Dad decided to take soon after his arrival at his new home. It was not something to be done lightly; he was always aware of the responsibility he had to give his viewers correct information and balanced views.

Just as he did a few years later with his tomatoes, he decided that a trial of organic versus inorganic would be required and all the data he collected should be recorded. This trial was carried out in what is now the orchard, where he set out three beds planted identically: two blackcurrant bushes, a gooseberry bush, an apple tree and a pear tree in each bed.

The idea behind the three-bed trial was to have one organic bed, one inorganic bed, and a control bed with nothing added so that he had something to gauge the other two against. In his allotment area he grew three rows of a selected range of veg – root, cucurbits, leafy, legumes, tubers and tomatoes – all using the same organic, non-organic and control methods. Not only would this three-year trial give him all the information he needed to make a properly educated decision about whether or not to garden completely organically, but it would also give his viewers food for thought.

He was keen to become organic but needed to make sure he was not leading viewers up a garden path on a whim or by his desire to do the right thing. As time passed it was clear that, as he had expected, both the organic and non-organic crops were producing far better than the control, but there was little difference between them.

Dad was meticulous in his recording and by the time he'd completed his third year of growing, his mind was made up: he was going to use only organic principles at Barnsdale. If there was little or no difference between organic and inorganic, there was obviously no advantage in being inorganic. His decision was not only for the fruit and veg areas at Barnsdale but the ornamental gardens too.

On the first *Gardeners' World* programme that was broadcast after this decision, he mentioned in passing that he was going to grow organically from then on. He didn't make a big thing about it; he was an educator, not a preacher. Viewers were aware of his trials because he'd mentioned them over the three years – but only because he liked to keep them informed about anything that could be valuable to them.

Although he didn't want to force organics onto his viewers, preferring them to make up their own minds, he was still very crafty in the way he approached the subject. With everything he did from that day onwards, if there was an organic and inorganic option he mentioned both, thus acknowledging that not all gardeners had become organic – but he always mentioned the organic method first in the hope that this would stick in the people's minds.

This move away from inorganic fertiliser and pesticides did not go down well with suppliers of those products that had been used by the presenters of *Gardeners' World* for years. The largest of them all railed against Dad's ideas and put out as much publicity as possible to counter the good work Dad was doing on *Gardeners' World*. Not only that, nearly all the employees of these companies who had been keen to liaise with him in the past no longer wanted to talk and made a concerted effort to ensure the horticultural industry, as well as the amateur gardener, continued down the inorganic route.

One person who worked for one of these large suppliers who remained a firm friend, was Gordon Rae. Since Dad passed away I have also become friendly with Gordon and his wife, Judith, and can fully understand why they stayed friends – such a lovely man!

This was not the outcome Dad had hoped for; he knew it would take time for the gardening public to change so there was still a place for both methods for many years to come. He was now a pariah for the horticultural chemicals industry but that didn't worry him; he wondered whether the suppliers had turned against his idea because, rather than wanting to learn about the unknown, they were scared of it.

Dad had foresight and was always looking for anything innovative that challenged his views. All he was doing was reverting to what we all did pre-chemicals and he saw this as an opportunity to change the way we did things, for the better – but unfortunately these companies did not seem to have the same opinion.

As it turned out, big businesses were not the only people he managed to upset. The Royal Horticultural Society took exception, something he had not intended.

One of Dad's commendable traits was that he liked things to be right. He was not obsessive but his practices reflected his familiar saying that 'if a job is worth doing then it's worth doing well' – not just well, but correctly too. When things were not done correctly and he felt the perpetrators should be held to account, he would tell them in such a pleasant way that often they didn't even realise he was doing it.

This was definitely *not* the case with the RHS, which at the time took umbrage with anyone questioning what they were doing. Although Dad had an inkling that all was not as it should be in his rather lax relationship with the Society, it was a while before he had an opportunity to ask a committee member why the RHS didn't like him. When the reply came, it was not what he was expecting: 'It's because you are a tabloid journalist.'

Dad thought some members were aloof, self-important and haughty, so the reply came as no great surprise. Thankfully these days things at the RHS have changed for the better.

Not satisfied with finding himself at the forefront of the organic movement in the UK, some years later Dad became aware of the destruction of our valuable peatlands. He'd been told that amateur gardeners were being supplied with large volumes of peat from important ecological sites; he needed to find out why and what could be done to prevent damage to the ecosystems that relied on them.

By then he was an experienced researcher, having researched many of the items for *Gardeners' World* programmes himself, so he was determined to find out what was happening.

When he did, he was horrified. In his opinion, the biggest UK compost supplier at the time was taking too big a proportion of its peat from Sites of Special Scientific Interest (SSSIs). The large peat-harvesting machinery was taking acres of this valuable habitat every day and destroying vital, internationally important habitats that had taken millions of years to create.

He vowed to get gardeners to use an alternative so peat-free gardening became his next mission. He had two hurdles to overcome: firstly, alternatives to peat-based composts were almost non-existent, and secondly, amateur gardeners were familiar with, and tended to rely on, peat composts.

Undaunted, he was fairly sure that he could find a way to convert those who were not for converting. As you would expect, he didn't jump in feet first; instead he set up a trial to see how newly developed coir composts compared with peat, adapting the way he dealt with these composts as he learned along the way.

As his trial progressed, the results were in line with what he expected with plusses and minuses for each type. To get a more accurate picture, he asked for my help to determine if we could develop a better coir mix that would be comparable with peat composts.

At the time the nursery was in its very early stages and I hadn't started to grow any plants, so we decided to use the early ornamental crops to try out different coir mixes. We found that the ones for rooting cuttings and seed sowing seemed to be very promising straight from the bags they came in, although I determined that early feeding was required. However, more work was needed to create a potting compost in order to get anywhere near the quality of growth generated by peat-based composts.

As a balance, Dad decided to trial the mixes I was using with his veg crops, bedding plants and the cuttings he'd taken that needed growing on to bigger plants before being planted in the garden.

Having trialled many different mixes, we eventually settled on a potting mix that seemed to work well with the widest range of crops. More than happy with the success of his peat-free compost mix, Dad set about converting as many gardeners as he could.

Since then, peat-free composts have developed and

are now primarily based on wood products, but Dad's foresight and understanding of the environmental issues attached to using peat were staggering; it has taken most of the horticultural industry more than twenty-five years to catch up.

We have continued our vision: we have only used peat-free compost in the nursery and the gardens for well over thirty years. Customers and visitors have told us innumerable times what excellent quality our nursery plants are and how great our veg area in the gardens looks!

Next, Dad applied environmentally-sound principles to items we used in our everyday lives and started to recycle. When I say he started recycling, it wasn't his first attempt; like all gardeners who produce their own compost, he'd been recycling for years as well as creating things using the 'make do-and-mend' principle. This time, however, he took it to another level: it was time to build a garden that would show viewers how beautiful one could be when created with the right reclaimed and recycled materials.

We soon realised how life had moved on in terms of how second-hand items were perceived and their cost. When I was a boy in the 1960s and 70s, we often went into second-hand shops to see what was for sale. These were not the charity shops we have today but businesses that bought and sold things people no longer needed at less than half the price that they would be new. Since the 1980s the term 'second-hand' has been replaced with 'reclaimed', a posher version that immediately gives the impression that items will also be more expensive.

Initially 'reclaimed' was used to label expensive statuary but soon it spread to almost anything that was second-hand and usable in a garden. The problem was that 'second-hand' gives the sense you are getting a second-class item; the posher name doesn't, and that allows sellers to push up the prices. Many items for sale at less than half the price when I was a child are now being sold for five times as much!

Dad became aware of this price inflation when he visited reclamation yards in search of materials. In one yard he found sections of beautiful wrought-iron fencing, a couple of York-stone paving slabs and a large stack of old floorboards. This sent his brain into a whirlwind of activity as to how they could be used.

The floorboards were perfect for creating the outer fencing of the garden, and according to the yard owner they had been removed from what he described as 'an asylum', so they were perfect for Dad. The York stone would form the main part of a small patio area, while the wrought-iron fencing would be placed at the front of the garden.

The yard owner mentioned that he had some old oak roofing timbers, and when Dad saw them he could immediately visualise their use. He needed height and was thinking about a pergola: these timbers would be perfect. The fact that they'd been rescued from a derelict cottage was even better because they would now rise up again.

Before he'd set off on his trip to the reclamation yard he'd been sure he would find some reclaimed railway sleepers, which would make perfect raised vegetable beds. Typically, he came home with many items he'd not set out to buy but the one thing they didn't have in stock were any railway sleepers! It became my job to find those.

Dad had a knack of being friendly with the right people, ones that you didn't expect him to get on with, and he would tap them for information, products or favours when he needed to. He was always gracious when contacting these business friends, particularly when he wanted something gratis, although he always had the option of bartering for whatever he needed with the fruit and veg he was growing.

On this occasion he had to contact his good friend Willie Brown, who had been a co-conspirator of the 'twinning with Paris group'. Dad had an idea for a water feature that would take pride of place in the garden; it would be created from an old immersion heater, which is where Willie Brown, who was a plumber, came in.

Dad had already found an artist's studio in Brighton that could create his vision, so it was just a case of waiting for someone who needed Willie to replace their immersion heater. Not wanting to miss an opportunity to save money, Dad not only managed to blag an old heater for a couple of handfuls of Brussels sprouts but also persuaded Willie Brown to part with the pipework he had removed with it for free!

Now that Dad had received all the parts he needed, he despatched them to the south coast. He also needed to involve our local blacksmith because the wrought-iron fencing was one panel short of the set needed to surround the front of the garden. He took a panel to the blacksmith and left him with instructions to make one as close to this reclaimed panel as he could.

The fencing returned within a couple of weeks and was erected once it had all been painted deep green. When the crew came to film shortly afterwards, Dad explained to the producer that he'd been one panel short and the process he'd gone through to have one made. When the producer asked which was the new panel, Dad couldn't tell him. That is how talented our local blacksmith was.

In due course the immersion heater and pipework returned too, completely transformed. The two artists had turned these everyday items into a fantastic copper rose fountain. Dad absolutely loved it, as did I; it added a massive visual impact to the garden as well as an audible one, and thirty years later it is something I still marvel at every time I pass the reclaimed garden.

It was easy to install. The base was fixed to a stand which sat inside a circular watertight container that had been sunk into the ground with a pump in the bottom; in effect, it was a large bucket with a pump. At soil level Dad placed a strong wire mesh covered with pebbles to hide the workings below. The pump recycled the water up the main stem of the rose fountain and out of the top, where it ran down the petals and back into the receptacle.

Dad knew that this visual and audible joy would divide people: some would absolutely love it as much as he did, others would find it an abomination. That was fine, because all he was asked to do was to give viewers ideas about what *they* could do. Everyone watching his programmes was different and he knew that he could not please all of the people all of the time.

He was now a man inspired as to what he could create with a bit of ingenuity and some household items, so he looked for other potential garden-worthy creations – and this was where his local lawnmower repair man became an integral part of one of his visions.

At the end of every summer, Dad took his lawnmowers into Oakham to the repair shop of Peter, our local lawnmower dealer. During the quieter months of his year, Peter had turned his hand to making small statues and models out of the second-hand lawnmower parts.

As Dad was standing in the doorway of the workshop, explaining what he thought needed doing to each of the three mowers he'd brought in, he noticed a lovely small statue of a soldier behind where Peter was standing.

He made an instant decision that something like that would be the perfect focal point at the top end of the reclaimed garden, something that would draw one's eye through the pergola. He asked Peter if he could make something similar but bigger: he wanted a statue that would stand about 1.2m (4ft) high and be made from recycled mechanical parts.

Although it was now coming up to his busiest time of year, Peter seemed excited about the project and keen to take it on. He was sure that it would be completed within the timescale he had been given.

Dad was a very happy chappy when he left, oblivious to the fact that in all the years he had been taking his lawnmowers to Peter for servicing and repair not one had been returned to him on time! When the deadline came and went, he made almost daily visits to see Peter to remind him.

After several weeks Peter arrived at Barnsdale in his Ford Escort van with his masterpiece wrapped in a blanket in the back. Once it was unwrapped, the joy on Dad's face was clear: it was even better than he'd envisaged.

He immediately carried the statue down to the reclaimed garden and placed it carefully on the paving slab he had installed for the purpose several weeks earlier. Peter scurried behind him then they both stood back, silently admiring the masterpiece which was framed perfectly by the oak pergola uprights.

Dad thanked Peter (probably more times than Peter had been thanked for anything he had ever done) then looked at the statue in greater detail. The figure was in a seated position (the seat was a lawnmower roller) and his legs were out in front of him and bent. You needed to look carefully to see how every part of this magnificent sculpture had been recycled from either a lawnmower or a tractor.

I'm sure that this was not done intentionally, but the thing that amazed me most was how Peter had captured Dad's very thin legs perfectly by using parts of a tractor three-point-linkage. It's a vivid image that appears in my head from time to time, particularly when I walk past the reclaimed garden, because I can no longer gaze through the pergola and enjoy the soldier statue. It is no longer there.

On a summer's morning in 2013, a distraught member of staff noticed that the statue had disappeared and came to ask me if it had been taken for repair. It hadn't: that night someone had entered the gardens and stolen it, together with two small bronze-cast hens.

This was not just a devastating event for me but for the whole staff at Barnsdale. The statue had become an integral, iconic part of the gardens and everyone had taken ownership of it. Though it is now missing, I don't think that has detracted from the visual experience of most of our visitors; the garden still looks fantastic and most people who come are first-time visitors who didn't even know it was there.

Sadly Peter is no longer with us either, so I cannot get an identical replacement. We've tried various alternative focal points but when you know what should be there, nothing else comes up to scratch. That's not surprising: not only was it the only statue of its kind in the world, it also had a perfect representation of my dad's legs!

The reclaimed garden was constructed in 1996, the same year as the Paradise Gardens, so Dad used recycling in the Country Paradise Garden, too. He used reclaimed paving for the patio, which also had drainage pipes set into it to act as planting pockets for very prostrate thymes. He didn't stop there because in one of his outbuildings he found a small stack of terracotta roof tiles that had obviously been left there by a former occupant. He decided to use them as a walkway from the patio into the nut walk. To make them look as effective as possible, he set them in mortar on their edges in a zig-zag pattern; not only do they look great, they are exceptionally hard wearing.

This stroke of luck with the roof tiles seemed to balance out the disappointment of the hermitage he wanted to feature in this series.

To a hermit, paradise is being shut away from everyone and everything. To satisfy his sense of humour and to add a bit of fun to this series, Dad hatched a plan that involved a BBC researcher scouring the country for a hermitage, which the team could then film. He would then show viewers how to build their own, if that was something they felt they needed. His tag line was that everyone needs somewhere to escape to at certain times in their lives, so why not build your own bolthole in your garden, somewhere you could retreat to for some 'me time' whenever it was needed?

He thought a hermitage would be easy to find, so

he confidently set about building his own DIY one. It would fit well into the woodland area of his garden and that dictated its style: very rustic, with a woodland hut feel to it.

Once he'd drawn up the plans, he started building it in his workshop. He created the inner shell first by using four fenceposts and attaching marine-quality plywood to create the back and two side walls. The front would have a stable door, again made with plywood, but he wanted his hermitage to be multifunctional so he cut out a rectangle in the top half of the stable door. This was hinged at the top to give him a flap that could be wedged open: the hermitage could now be used as a bird hide, too!

He attached half logs to the outside of the walls and the two halves of the door, and bundles of twigs to the plywood roof to give the structure a wooden-hut look. He put a bolt to close his bird-viewing flap and two bolts on his stable door: one inside to keep the two halves together so that it could be used as a single door and one to lock the door from the outside.

The hermitage was now complete. Having already decided where he would place it, it was ready to be moved into his woodland area.

It was several weeks since he'd asked the BBC researcher to find a hermitage for them to film and the task had turned out to be anything but simple. Just as Dad had resigned himself to removing the hermitage from the series, unexpectedly the researcher came up trumps – or so Dad thought. She'd scoured the country up, down, sideways and diagonally, and eventually discovered a hermitage only twenty-four miles from Barnsdale at Belvoir Castle.

Dad was chuffed to bits, not only because one had been found but because it was local. He showed me the exact spot where he wanted to position his home-made hermitage then went off with the crew to film, leaving me to muster a couple of our chaps to move his construction into its woodland home.

Having experienced thirty-three years of Geoff Hamilton constructions I should have known better, but it was not until we had staggered about twenty paces that I realised why he'd dashed off so quickly: this thing weighed an absolute tonne. Not only had he used 2cm (¾inch) thick plywood for the walls and roof, but he'd attached half a forest to the side of it. The only surprising part about moving it was that none of us suffered a double hernia!

As with all his constructions, he'd made this one to last. In the event of a nuclear missile landing on Rutland, there is no question that the gardens at Barnsdale would be completely flattened but this hermitage would still be standing!

We'd not even had time to catch our breath after our mammoth hermitage-moving effort when Dad reappeared, presumably having finished filming at Belvoir Castle. In stark contrast to when he'd left, he seemed despondent and I wondered if the filming had gone as well as I'd initially assumed.

I was almost spot on. The crew set up for filming but when Dad arrived to extol the virtues of being a hermit, it turned out that this hermitage was actually a summerhouse – a very nice summerhouse but not the hermitage he needed. His beautifully constructed home-made hermitage never did feature in the *Paradise Gardens* series.

It turned out not to be a completely fruitless trip, however, because he returned with a wonderfully structured piece of tree root that Belvoir Castle head gardener had given him, which he asked me to place in the woodland, close to the hermitage.

When I asked if it would be as heavy as the construction we'd just man-handled into the woodland, he called me a 'spowpeen' and told me to get on with it.

I have researched this word to see if it was one that he made up, as some of his sayings were, or whether it is a bona-fide word. The closest I could get was 'spalpeen' and I think this was the word he wanted. That also means being a rascal, although he had changed its meaning to suit his parental requirements!

Chapter Twelve

In the latter years of his filming life, things changed. The BBC seemed to be becoming more insular and harder to work with, and it was more difficult to make the quality programmes Dad was used to.

Over the years his producers on *Gardeners' World* had wanted their relationship with Dad to be a partnership. They worked together to produce the best programme they possibly could by merging their specialities: Dad the gardening expert, and the producer the programme-making expert. John Kenyon had hit the nail on the head when they'd first started filming at Barnsdale and he'd said, 'Now, Geoff, you are the gardening expert and I am the television expert. You tell me what needs doing and how it is done, and I will tell you the best way to film it. Together we will make the best gardening programme there has ever been'.

Sadly, Dad felt that this ideology had disappeared and the new breed of producers were not using his expertise as much as they should, bearing in mind his standing in the horticultural world and that he was a fountain of information and ideas. He started to feel that viewers were getting get a raw deal and not being given the easy-to-understand practical information they craved.

The conversations we'd had periodically since I'd started at horticultural college about eventually setting up a little business together became more frequent, partly because of his disillusionment with the future of *Gardeners' World*, and because of the plant nursery idea gradually being developed. It looked like we'd work together producing plants for sale and cultivating the extra garden space around the nursery rather than me doing all the work and him providing the money to enable me to continue.

It came as no surprise when he started dropping 'when I retire from the television' into conversations about the nursery. However, he never made it clear when this might be because his retirement schedule seemed to be dependent on what sort of filming day he'd had. If he spent all day dealing with a producer whom he felt was not up to scratch or who would not listen to his horticultural advice, that evening he would talk about retiring in a matter of weeks. If by some stroke of luck he had a producer who wanted to work with him and create the Barnsdale sections of the programme as Dad knew they should be, then he talked about filming indefinitely. The reality was that he didn't know when he would retire – and neither did we!

For me, the most important thing was that he was talking about retirement so we needed a plan in place as to how we would move forward once the television work ended. After much discussion, Dad decided that on retirement he would section off a small part of the garden closest to his house so that he could still satisfy his gardening desires and the rest would be open to the public as an extension of the nursery garden.

Although the development of the nursery garden area would keep him occupied for a few years, he wanted something he could return to after his 'second' retirement. Rather than having an honesty box on the nursery-garden gatepost, we would charge an admission fee to view both the nursery and television gardens. We discussed this while looking at a rough plan he'd drawn up of the two adjoining areas. I noted from his tone and gestures that his idea of a 'small part of the garden' was significantly different to mine, but I am sure that when the time came we would have come to some sort of compromise.

The date seemed to ebb and flow like the English Channel, but I still felt that this momentous retirement was some way off so I didn't take the plan any further, intending to revisit it in two- or three-years' time. However, a short while later in the early spring of 1995, something happened that made me return the plan to a prominent place on my desk for review.

It was early Friday morning and I'd been in stealth mode, wandering the television garden looking for propagation material, when I noticed the film crew had finished setting up and were waiting for Dad to appear. As filming had not started, I went to say hello and have a quick chat. Out of the corner of my eye, I saw that week's producer returning from a brief walk around the garden. I knew that she had not encountered Dad because he was at the opposite end of the garden preparing a piece of ground for sowing hardy annuals, the subject of the film sequence. She asked if anyone had seen him. This was her first time at Barnsdale and she didn't know me, so I introduced myself and cut short my conversation with the crew to take her to Dad.

As we walked, I saw that she was clutching a handful of papers which I assumed were her notes for that day's filming. Dad told me that I was not needed for anything, so I left them to it. I heard them introduce themselves but something she said made me turn to see her thrust a paper in Dad's direction.

I had an inkling that all was not as it should be so I hung back. I didn't want to interfere – and that turned out to be absolutely the right decision. I couldn't hear what they were saying but I could see that Dad was turning very red. I swear that I could see steam coming out of his ears.

He thrust the paper back into the producer's hands, said a few words, turned and walked away very quickly then disappeared. He didn't return for well over half an hour, by which time his face had returned to its normal colour. He beckoned the producer away from the rest of the BBC crew and they spoke quietly for a minute or two before going back to the crew to start filming. I went back into the garden.

As I usually did at the end of the day, I popped up to see Dad to fill him in on my day on the nursery as well as to satisfy my curiosity about the moment his head had looked like it was about to explode. It turned out that the paper the producer had thrust into his hand was a script for him to learn about the tasks he was about to perform.

To say that this was not appreciated would have been the understatement of 1995. Dad was absolutely fuming that they considered he needed a script and had given him something that he felt had been written by someone two or three years out of college was the final straw. I understood his frustration: I knew – and he knew – that not only was he the top television gardening presenter of his generation, but he also had more than forty years of horticultural experience!

He was still very cross and determined that it would not happen again. I tried to find out what he'd said to the producer but he wouldn't tell me, only that she understood that he would not work from a prepared script.

This was a seminal moment for Dad when he recognised that things had changed and it left him with only one option: he needed to get away from *Gardeners' World*.

Having discussed the events of that Friday morning, he quickly moved on to a couple of ideas he'd had for a new weekly series that he could write and present for the BBC and, importantly, one where he'd have greater content control. He wasn't a control freak but he wanted to ensure that the gardening public got what they needed and, having been right for more than sixteen years, he knew he was in tune with his audience. It was amazing how quickly great ideas seemed to flow into his head.

One of his greatest ideas was to have a flower show in the Midlands. He already had a close relationship with the Chelsea Flower Show (that he continued to enjoy for the rest of his life), but he also attended the Hampton Court Palace Flower Show each year, as well as occasionally visiting the RHS flower shows in their Vincent Square halls. All of these shows were in London, although there were others in the north of the country such as the Harrogate Flower Show in spring and autumn, the Malvern Flower Show twice a year, the Shrewsbury Flower Show, and the Sandringham Flower Show in the east during July – but there were no big flower shows in central England. This was about to change.

Dad knew that there were a lot of gardeners in the Midlands who had to travel many miles to enjoy a flower show. He knew how great these shows were with their many exhibitors providing a range of plants and garden accessories that you would never find in one place anywhere else. There was no way that he could put on a show himself, so there was only one thing left for him to do: pitch his idea to a company specialising in that sort of thing.

Although they weren't involved with flower shows, BBC Exhibitions were old hands at staging other exhibitions. Wanting to keep it in the family, as it were, he thought they would be the best people to pitch his idea to.

They didn't need convincing, absolutely loved the idea and were keen to be a big part of this new venture. Dad, with others, started to drive the concept forward; he was adamant that the show should start big to meet demand, so they decided that the National Exhibition Centre (NEC) could provide the space and facilities they needed. That was fine for some of the exhibitors, but plants need light and being inside was not ideal.

After a lot of initial planning, Dad became less involved; the BBC Exhibitions team had far more experience in setting up these events and he had gardening to get back to.

The team had managed to secure a sponsor so, much to everyone's relief, the financial liability was nullified but disaster struck a few months before the show was due to open as the main sponsor pulled out and panic ensued. Many companies were contacted to see if they would step up as the main show sponsor but without success until someone approached the Express Newspaper office and proposed they did it. Unsurprisingly, they leapt at the opportunity because, at the time, Dad was the gardening writer in the Saturday edition of the *Daily Express*. What was surprising was that nobody had thought of contacting them first! This enthusiasm included a desire for Dad to build the main feature garden at the show. What could he say to that, bearing in mind that they had just rescued his baby? He said exactly what he should, a resounding 'yes'.

He was now committed to producing a garden that would be the main showpiece of the whole show but that did not faze him. Having built gardens at the Chelsea Flower Show, he was a seasoned show garden designer and builder – but he was also a very busy man. He thought long and hard; it was a difficult decision to pass the design and build job to someone else, but who?

Fortunately he'd come across a brilliant young designer, Dan Pearson, at the Chelsea Flower Show the previous year and he, in Dad's opinion, was just the person for the job. When Dan agreed to take it on, Dad told him the sort of show garden he wanted to create. He knew that he was on to a winner with Dan so he stepped back and let him get on with what he knew would be the perfect showpiece for this inaugural event.

Bearing in mind that the show was due to open on Wednesday 13th June, it only took until the end of April for Dad to mention to me that Dan might need some of my home-grown plants for his display. I always loved the way he was so casual with some of his requests – and so imprecise; when he said a few, he didn't mention that ultimately Dan would fill two removal lorries with plants from my nursery!

These were transported to the NEC in an Exton Removals lorry, not only because they were a local company but also because Dad knew the owner, Jim Footit, and managed to get a really good price!

I was bemused by how many plants were needed. I had only created much smaller displays in floral marquees, so it was not until I moved up a gear and started to put on larger displays myself that I learned the joy of having the best selection of plants to choose from.

Dan didn't just use my plants; he had ordered the bulk from a couple of much bigger nurseries so his creative planting juices were able to flow unabated. The plants he didn't use were returned. As we have become accustomed to from a Dan Pearson creation, the show garden was fantastic and wowed all the visitors who had the pleasure of seeing it.

At the end of a phenomenally successful first *Gardeners' World* Live, our job was to dismantle the show garden and ship it out of the hall. You only get one day to do this because the NEC usually has another event planned. As it turned out, by lunchtime the following day everything had been taken apart and was stacked on pallets ready to be moved out.

Dad contacted the *Daily Express* to see where they wanted the materials and plants sending and they gave him an unexpected reply. They had paid for every element of that garden, so you'd have thought they would be pleased to receive what they had paid for but instead they asked, 'What do we want with a garden? We are in offices in London. Can you not dispose of them elsewhere?'

Surprised as he was by this reply, Dad didn't argue. He put down the phone and immediately phoned Jim Footit. His removal lorry arrived first thing the following morning and was loaded and back at Barnsdale by lunchtime. What a great way to get a complete garden for just £50 – the cost of the lorry to bring it home.

Dad wanted the show to be much more visitor focused, friendly and, most of all, more personal, so having all the *Gardeners' World* presenters in attendance and accessible was crucial. To him, great as it was to listen to presenters from a flower-show stage, he wanted visitors to be able to talk to them on the floor of the show.

It was a great idea. Though he returned to his on-site hotel each evening absolutely shattered, he woke up the following morning reinvigorated and looking forward to meeting a new batch of *Gardeners' World* viewers.

I am sure that the couple of gin and tonics he enjoyed at the bar the evening before helped with that enthusiasm, but nothing really matched his love of meeting and talking to people, particularly those who wanted to talk gardening. Best of all, at this very first *Gardeners' World Live* flower show, he had plenty of time between his pre-arranged appearances at various stands around the showground and that gave him the opportunity to talk to more people than he could count!

This did not go unnoticed by the show's team; when he received his show schedule for the following year, there were a lot more pre-arranged appearances. By the third year, things had moved to another level and he was pretty much finishing one appearance and moving on to the next to fit them all in. His schedule was like this from the time the show opened until it shut and was repeated every day. That was problematic for Dad because it went against everything he felt the show should be, but he had to accept that he was the main draw and though he was the inspiration for the show, he was not the organiser.

Even so, he was sure that there was a way around this problem and within an hour of the first day he had found it. When he finished an appearance on a particular stand he talked to one or two people who were waiting for him, then pointed in whatever direction he need to walk to his next appearance. 'I need to be over there in a couple of minutes, so if you want to talk to me then please walk with me.'

It was the perfect line; he was like the Pied Piper meandering around the showground but, most importantly, he fulfilled his commitments on his schedule as well as to the people who wanted to chat to him. It really didn't matter if they wanted an answer to a gardening problem or whether they just wanted to say that they had spoken to Geoff Hamilton; he was very much a gardener of the people and it was all part of his job, whether he was being paid for it or not.

He found the show and the other personal appearances around the country quite tiring, and it used to take him a day or two to recover. That was sad because, in order to continue presenting on *Gardeners' World* from Barnsdale he had no choice but to take on extra work to pay the bills. He was never one to shy away from work but he had to overload himself with it to keep Barnsdale afloat. The BBC didn't contribute anywhere near enough for most of the years he presented from Barnsdale, so in order to stay on television he funded the place from his own pocket.

Although the money from the BBC increased over the years, it never covered all his costs. It was a pity that the majority of BBC executives didn't appreciate what they had in Barnsdale and what a jewel their main presenter was to them and their viewers.

This was clearly highlighted when he was asked by the *Daily Express* if he would have a photograph taken standing in front of his local newsagent's shop with a copy of the newspaper in his hands. It would be a mocked-up newspaper because they wanted to promote a seed packet offer that was coming up in a few weeks' time. As Dad was their gardening writer, he was the perfect person for this picture.

He had no problem with the proposal; the more gardening readers they attracted the better it would be for him and the horticultural industry. However, mindful of doing the right thing, he said he would need to get clearance from the BBC. The following day he telephoned the BBC for what he thought would be a quick confirmation that it would be fine but the person he spoke to couldn't make that sort of decision. They needed to ask someone else and would phone Dad back as soon as they had an answer.

After a couple of days the person from the BBC called to tell him exactly what he wanted to hear: there was no problem with him having his picture taken to promote an edition of the *Daily Express*.

This was great news, but Dad began to wonder why the person he was speaking to had paused. Just as he was about to thank them, they continued; with hindsight he realised that the long pause was probably a minor employee steeling themselves before they delivered another piece of news.

'I have heard back from the relevant BBC department. They have absolutely no problem with you having your picture taken by *Daily Express* to promote the free seed-packet offer, but if you do so you will be sacked.'

It was such an amazing statement, put in such an amazing way to their top television presenter, that it came as a massive shock. It was an eye-opener, too.

Dad was not often lost for words but on this occasion he really couldn't think of any. He gave a bemused sigh before thanking the person on the other end of the phone and ringing off.

It was not the fact that they had refused his request, it was the way in which they had conveyed the decision as if he meant nothing to the BBC. In the few minutes after that phone call he realised exactly how the Corporation must view him and how dispensable he was in their eyes.

There is no question that if the BBC had sacked him there would have been an outcry, with gardeners from all over the country descending on the BBC's London offices, dibbers in hand, to protest until he was reinstated! But it showed the complete lack of respect they had for their top gardening presenter and it was a real wake-up call.

Dad believed in the BBC as a British institution of quality. He had worked hard to achieve the best he could on the very limited budget they gave him, even travelling the length and breadth of the country himself to research his programmes. He'd gone all over the United Kingdom to talk to horticultural experts who'd been earmarked to appear on the programme, as well as amateurs whose gardens might make a good feature. Whenever possible, he asked for products and equipment to be sent to him to test out before featuring them but occasionally he had to travel to fetch what he wanted.

He usually left both amateur and professional guests feeling positive about how they would come across on the programme, and most of the time his trust was well-founded. There were times when he visited someone after an initial telephone conversation, having deemed them suitable for the programme, and his hopes were realised when he met them. If they came across as outgoing and easy to talk to (although sometimes difficult to stop!), he would suggest them to the producer who booked them in for filming.

Dad would return on the scheduled day with a film crew and producer in tow and be greeted by the same person he had encountered a few weeks before. Once the camera was set up and the sound man had fitted the microphones, Dad and the producer went through what they intended to do and say and what they would like from the guest. Everything was agreed and everyone confirmed that they were happy, so they took up their positions the camera started to roll and Dad started talking.

Sometimes, however, when it came to the guest's turn to speak it was like someone had glued their lips together or they'd swallowed a dictionary of gobbledygook. When the camera was pointed in their direction, they couldn't get a coherent sentence out of their mouths. On such rare occasions, the production team still made the most of where they were and continued with Dad waxing lyrical about the garden without the owner being filmed. He found it odd that pointing a piece of equipment at someone would turn their legs to jelly, but then he was used to it.

While he was away filming these programme inserts, things were being prepared at Barnsdale for the next filming session by two full-time staff, one part-timer and one office person who also did some gardening when the office was quiet.

The pressures of weekly filming combined with his writing obligations meant that Dad's only option was to reserve the weekends as his own gardening time. He loved nothing more than getting out of the office and being in his beloved garden, and joyfully carried out any task that needed completing – which is why the position of his office always seemed strange to me. When converting the old hay loft in his barn into two offices, why did he put his secretary in the back office while he took up residence in the front office? Each office had a window with a desk in front, so while his secretary had the pleasure of looking out onto his driveway, he looked out over his garden. It must have been torture for him to look at the place he really wanted to be knowing that he had to stay where he was and finish what he considered by far the less enjoyable part of his work.

There are two ways to look at this odd situation: either he felt the need to suffer every time he looked out of the window, or it was a clever ploy. He was an ideas' person and gazing onto a beautiful garden helped this process; it was obviously a greater source of inspiration than looking at the driveway. I could see his point. Also, looking out over the place you wanted to be could spur you on to finish your work faster – though unfortunately it had no effect on speeding up his two-fingered typing!

I've been an employer for about half my life and I've gone down the same route as Dad in the way that I do things. I remember that at college 90% of my horticultural group had the same aim: to be self-employed. They misguidedly believed that this meant you could do what you wanted when you wanted, and if you didn't fancy working on a particular day you didn't have to. That was – and still is – an unrealistic view because when you're self-employed you generally work twice as long as everyone else.

One thing about being self-employed that I could not understand with Dad was that he had to manufacture reasons to take himself out of his office and into the garden. I always felt that this was why he wrote his three mini-series, *The Ornamental Kitchen Garden*, *Geoff Hamilton's Cottage Gardens* and *Geoff Hamilton's Paradise Gardens*: they were a means of getting him out of the office and into the garden. Then I remember that I have also found myself deciding that, even though I have a more than capable workforce, certain jobs could only be done by me. Like Dad, I feel obliged to find jobs to get me out of the office as opposed to getting out of my office chair and leaving because I can.

Mind you, Dad's desire to get into the garden to do as much as he could did not stop him taking credit for work he had *not* done. It did not happen often but, when it did, it was obvious that he had honed the art of 'taking all the credit' over many years and now considered himself a master.

Not long after I moved in with Dad and started to work with him at Barnsdale full-time, he had an idea about how to grow a wide range of top fruit within a restricted space that would make an excellent feature on *Gardeners' World*. He had seen various Laburnum and Wisteria tunnels and thought this type of feature would look just as good with apple and pear trees growing over several arches that had been made into a tunnel. On this particular occasion he didn't write anything down because he had the vision in his head.

Having measured the area where he wanted to put the tunnel, he was certain it would not only fit but also look great; the feature would be stunning and the view through it would be on to arable fields. He knew that Agriframes made a relatively cheap two-hoop arch and sold extension kits so he could add as many hoops as his space allowed.

He ordered the arch and thirteen extensions, plus a range of bare-root apple and pear trees. At that point I got involved, having been given the task of cultivating the ground and raking it level. When the arches arrived, I set about erecting them and joining them together then I laid the turf, something I'd done many times before so I knew that the finished grass area would pass the critical eye of my employer – after all, it was he who had had taught me many years previously!

Dad had ordered one each of twenty-four different varieties of apple, and two of each of three varieties of pear. When they arrived, my final job was to plant one against each upright of each hoop. I had left an ungrassed bed running along the bottom of the arches to facilitate the tree planting so that the apples and pears could go on the outside of the tunnel.

I should have realised what was going to happen when I was asked to plant all the trees except for the very last one on the right-hand side of the very last hoop. Filming was the following day and I was despatched to another part of the garden so that I didn't disturb the process.

When I sat down a week later to watch *Gardeners' World* there it was: the apple-arch tunnel that I had erected surrounded by the beautiful lush, green turf that I had laid so professionally, and finished off by the range of cordon apples and pears beautifully tied to each arch.

With the exception of the one at the end.

There I sat, proudly basking in the glory of my handiwork, when Dad appeared and announced that now he had finished erecting the tunnel, laying the turf and planting the trees, he only had one left to do. My jaw hit the floor; if I'd had anyone there to speak to, I'm sure I'd have been rendered speechless!

I'm positive that the reason I can't remember Dad's response to the question I posed about the authenticity of his comment is due to the trauma I endured that Friday evening. However, I've recounted this story to hundreds of people over the years, which shows that it had no lasting effect on me and that I'm not bitter!

Chapter Thirteen

Having become disillusioned with the garden path *Gardeners' World* seemed to be taking him down, Dad felt he needed to move onto something else that would enable him to educate and enthuse other gardeners the Geoff Hamilton way.

This could be another gardening programme, though not one to compete with *Gardeners' World*; no, this one would complement the existing programmes. Having come up with the idea, he had to cope with the tsunami of ideas that then flooded his brain. What he needed to do was to make a scribbled note of each one then go back to the beginning and start with the programme format. He was determined not to trip up by running before he could walk.

To complement *Gardeners' World* his new programme would have to be a BBC production, which was fine because all his television contacts were at the BBC. He was keen for it to be significantly different though, and, by drawing on his seventeen years of presenting experience, he understood what he needed to do. It would be more of a consumer magazine type of programme where he could carry out trials of tools, machinery and growing techniques – but God forbid no tomatoes this time! There would be space to look at new products and innovations that would benefit gardeners and to visit places that *Gardeners' World* would never consider going.

To Dad it was all about filling in the gaps but not falling foul of the BBC regulations on advertising, so he'd have to make sure the budget allowed for lots of black tape to blank out company names on products.

He knew what he had to do to get this programme commissioned because he'd been though that wringer three times before, with the *Ornamental Kitchen Garden, Cottage Gardens* and *Paradise Gardens* series. He developed his presentation, making sure that all the 'I's' were dotted and all the 'T's' were crossed, before attending a meeting with a BBC executive. It went well; the executive seemed impressed with the idea and format and felt (as Dad already knew) that it would enhance their flagship gardening programme and draw in more viewers to the BBC.

There was always a process to go through and Dad wasn't expecting to hear from the BBC for at least two weeks. Four weeks later he received a phone call from the executive he'd met who said he'd gone to his superiors with Dad's proposition and they also felt that it was worthy. They were prepared to give it a run of twelve programmes on BBC2 to see how it went; in fact, they were so keen that they would put it in a daytime slot!

I was completely gobsmacked when Dad told me, but nowhere near as gobsmacked as he'd been when they'd told him the planned timing to broadcast his new programme.

He was far too modest to comment, but I was not. 'How can they put the most popular gardening presenter there's ever been in a daytime slot and not the prime-time evening slot this programme deserves?' I demanded.

With the help of his first two *Gardeners' World* producers and those who had produced his three short series, he had quadrupled the viewing figures of *Gardeners' World* and taken it to heights these BBC executives could only have dreamt of. I was staggered but Dad took it in his stride. He told the executive that he would work on the series so that it would be ready to go once he'd finished filming the *Paradise Gardens* series that was already in production.

Filming *Geoff Hamilton's Paradise Gardens* had started well but then disaster struck. While Dad was being filmed laying paving in the Paradise Town Garden, he began to feel unwell. It must have been bad because he decided to go back to the house to sit down.

He never took much notice of illness and generally worked through whatever life threw at him, but this seemed different. He suffered some chest pain and shortness of breath as he walked up the garden to the house, things he had not encountered before.

Lynda was so concerned about his condition that she

immediately phoned the local GP who came straight out and gave Dad a once over. It was not good news, and he was rushed to Leicester General Hospital with a suspected heart attack.

Once all the tests had been completed, the diagnosis was confirmed. Dad stayed in hospital for three days while they continued to monitor his situation and I have to say that, by the time he was ready for release back into the community, the nurses were pleased to see him go! He was not a good patient. From his arrival, he was pleading and pushing to be allowed back home, telling the medical staff that he would recuperate much better there, but it seemed that he was the only one who realised that he would get better if he could get back to his garden. He most certainly was not for lying in a bed for days when there was work to be done; more importantly, he was holding up the filming of his best series yet.

Eventually his wish was granted and he returned home with strict instructions about what he could do and when he was allowed to do it. The main thing he complained to me about was not the restrictions placed on physical work but the ban on eating cheese because of its high fat content. As you would expect from a committed cheese connoisseur, he resisted this demand with all the strength he could muster.

When his heart specialist realised that the cheese embargo was not going to work, he moved on to what he felt was a happy medium: instead of a total cheese ban, Dad could eat the half-fat versions of his favourite types. Dad and I both knew that half the fat meant that the cheese would be half as nice, and he was certainly not happy. Each lunchtime consisted of fresh bread and cheese so how would he cope? That was his main concern when I asked how he was feeling.

In fact, after only a few weeks he had settled into the regime of half-fat cheese and never again mentioned what he initially perceived as the catastrophic aftershock of suffering a mild heart attack.

Our next father-and-son discussion was about a calamity waiting to happen. A couple of weeks after he had emerged from hospital, he spoke to me again – but this time there was no mention of full-fat Brie or Camembert. Instead this conversation centred on his last Will and testament.

He had just returned from having it written and witnessed, so it was now legally binding, and he seemed intent on talking me through its contents and how they would impact me. I really wasn't interested in knowing what he had left me because, as far as I was concerned, he was now fine so his Will wouldn't be read for many years to come, by which time I would probably have forgotten all the detail.

I have always believed that nobody has a God-given right to anything; it is up to the owner to decide where their possessions are distributed and this should only be discovered at the reading of the Will. If Dad wanted to leave everything to Moss, his faithful border collie,

I would have been as happy as if he'd left it all to me.

He took no notice of my protests and decided to tell me anyway; once that was done, he went back to his office. A month or so later, when I was on a trip with him to a trade show, the subject must still have been on his mind because he started to talk very seriously about his funeral. His wishes had been detailed in his Will so legally they had to be carried out to the letter.

Dad had always been keen on New Orleans style funerals, the ones with a trumpeter leading the funeral cortege and all mourners singing and dancing behind it, and that was what he wanted for himself. That would be easy enough to arrange, although I wasn't sure how the sleepy, thatched-cottage village of Exton would take it. Dad was clear that he wanted it to be a celebration of his life as opposed to focusing on his death. He wanted happiness. Even though the topic was rather morbid, it was in keeping with driving on the horrific M6. However, things were just about to get quite hairy – just like driving on the M6!

He was aware that I had no experience or knowledge of the legalities involved with a person's Will and he used this to his advantage. He told me that by putting his requirements in his Will, my two brothers and I had to follow them precisely even though none of us were executors. Then he moved on to the coffin and burial.

Because he was talking about his funeral, at no point did it dawn on me that the Hamilton sense of humour was playing a part. Apparently, if we disobeyed his last wish all three of us would suffer hellfire, damnation, plague and subsequent starvation. Keeping a perfectly straight face he stated that he wanted his coffin to be plain, standard size with no frills but he wanted the hole it would go into to be slightly smaller than usual. He wanted it narrower and shorter than the standard measurements so that the coffin was the same size as the hole and the vicar would have to jump up and down on it to get it to slide to the bottom. He was grinning so much; to Dad that just had to be the perfect send off! I was horrified at the thought.

Satisfied that he had passed on his wishes for his final farewell, we carried on to the trade show and then back home, where life returned to normal.

He returned to writing the format for his new BBC2 series, but there was one thing he couldn't forget. To say that he was disappointed with the obvious lack of confidence in his seventeen years presenting *Gardeners' World*, as well as the three very successful mini-series he had written and presented for the BBC, was an understatement. But although he was gutted, he pulled up his socks and did what he always did: got on with it and drew up a plan of action for each programme in the run they had given him.

Unfortunately he was not destined to leave *Gardeners' World* and take the helm of his new daytime series because the problem with his heart resurfaced, this time in a devastating way. He had been at the forefront of so many environmental issues, so when Sustrans asked him to take part in a charity cycle ride to promote the need for more cycle tracks around the country, he couldn't refuse.

This event was taking place in Wales at the beginning of August on a cycle track in the Brecon Beacons National Park. It not only pressed his environmental button, it also tied into his new-found enjoyment of cycling. He had been only a very occasional rider but this changed when his heart specialist told him to do some gentle cycling to build up his strength and stamina after his first heart attack. He took this advice and decided to implement it as soon as he could, so it was no surprise to Lynda when, just a week after coming out of hospital, he told her that he was going out for a cycle ride and wouldn't be long.

Between getting home from hospital and his first venture out on his Raleigh, he ensured that someone cleaned off the cobwebs and sent it to the local cycle shop to be serviced. Once he started to pedal, he felt that his money had been well spent; his machine scooted along with very little effort on his part.

When he got to the end of his driveway he turned left to take the country route past Exton and on to Whitwell before turning back and coming home; it was a round trip of roughly two miles, which he felt was ideal to ease him into his new exercise regime.

When he reached the grass triangle on the edge of Exton he felt fine and was not breathing more heavily than normal. He took an executive decision that this was not far enough to be classed as proper exercise and decided to cycle another mile.

He set off towards Empingham, intending to turn around and head home when he met the Empingham Road on the other edge of Exton.

Having been confined to barracks for so long, it was a real joy to be out in the countryside with the birds singing and summer in full flow. He was so pleased to be feeling good that he decided not to turn round when he reached the Empingham Road but to go further on the road that headed towards the A1.

He'd been gone a while and Lynda was getting concerned. Dad hadn't returned from his short ride and, as he didn't have a mobile phone, she couldn't contact him to make sure everything was okay. All she could do was sit and worry, hoping that he had not collapsed into a ditch somewhere; she didn't even know in which direction he'd gone because he hadn't told her.

He was blissfully unaware of the worry he was causing as he took in his surroundings. He was so busy enjoying the scenery and bird song that he didn't notice how far he had pedalled until he realised that he was breathing quite heavily.

He finally stopped and looked around; the adjacent road was extraordinarily busy. He had cycled so far that he was now on the Lincolnshire side of the A1 and too far away to pedal home in his tired state.

Lynda was still pacing up and down the hallway when the landline phone rang. She looked at it, wondering if it was the emergency services or a hospital doctor calling her with bad news about Dad, then tentatively picked up the receiver. Relieved to hear Dad's panting voice at the other end, she breathed a huge sigh of relief.

Dad had knocked on the door of the nearest house, which happened to be occupied by an avid *Gardeners' World* viewer who was more than happy to let him to use their phone. He asked Lynda to jump in the Land Rover and collect both him and his bike.

As you would expect from his viewer, while Dad was waiting he was treated to a comfy chair to rest his weary bones and a hot cup of strong tea and accompanying biscuit. He was deep in conversation when there was a knock at the door and there was Lynda, his 'knight in shining armour'.

Dad's host put the bike into the back of the Land Rover and Dad and Lynda returned to the sanctuary of Barnsdale, where he was instructed to put his feet up for the rest of the day. He had learned his lesson and spent the rest of his recuperation cycling up and down the mile-long avenue.

On the morning of 3rd August, he spent an hour oiling all the moveable parts on his bike so that his machine was in full working order for the big Sustrans ride the following day. He put it in the back of the Land Rover together with their overnight bag, and he and Lynda headed off to the hotel in Wales that they had booked for the next couple of nights.

When they arrived after a long drive, Dad wasn't

feeling his best and decided to have a rare, late-afternoon rest before going down for their evening meal. Once they were back in the room, he still wasn't feeling great; if he felt the same the following morning, he'd have no option but to pull out of the event.

The following morning, the sun was filtering through the gaps in the curtains and it looked as if it would be a lovely day. Dad's spirits lifted to the point where, even though he was not feeling one hundred percent, he decided to fulfil his promise. It wasn't that he wanted to cycle up and down the Brecon Beacons for fun but his participation had been heavily publicised and he didn't want to let people down. He told himself, as most of us do from time to time, that he'd be fine once he got going.

Lynda dropped him off at the starting point and confirmed the approximate time of arrival at the finishing point, then drove off to enjoy the beauty that the Brecon Beacons National Park has to offer.

She arrived early at the finishing point and found several people milling around as they prepared the drinks and nibbles for the riders' return. Shortly after her arrival, a member of the Sustrans team came to find her to give her the news she'd been dreading ever since Dad had been diagnosed with his first heart attack. He had collapsed during the ride; although a paramedic had attended to him very quickly, his heart attack was so severe that he was probably dead before he hit the ground.

Bearing in mind how bad a patient he'd been during his first heart attack, it was the best way for him to go – though I'm sure he would have preferred to have fallen off his spade.

As he did with everything, he undoubtedly gave this ride his all and was enjoying the company of other cyclists on what turned out to be a perfect cycling day. During events like this it is human nature for us to see others around us without really taking notice of the detail, so nobody riding with Dad can tell me if he was smiling when the time came. The picture on the back cover of this book was taken only minutes before and, as you can see, he had a broad grin – but that's what he always had when somebody pointed a camera in his direction. I like to think that he went out with a typically Geoff Hamilton grin on his face

Neither my two brothers nor I had seen a dead body before, so when the opportunity came to visit Dad at the local funeral parlour I was uncertain whether to go or not. When Cyril had died, Mum had asked me if I wanted to go with her to see him laid out and I'd turned down the offer. I was only seventeen and couldn't understand the reasoning behind such an act.

However, my younger brother Chris and I decided to visit Dad. We arranged to meet in Oakham so that we could go together and give each other support. We weren't sure how we would react, although we were clear that we would each visit Dad alone and have our own time with him. It turned out to be an extraordinarily cathartic thing for both of us that lifted the intense feelings of loss and grief. I have not felt those emotions every day since, but that visit made them more bearable.

Part of that catharsis was because of the person who had laid him out. On our way back to the car park, my brother and I agreed that the person who'd tended him must have done so with Dad's *Cottage Garden* book in one hand because Dad had exactly the same pose and the same grin that he has on the front of the book.

Our mood turned more positive; we could look back with immense pride at Dad's incredible achievements. He'd spent his life – certainly the last twenty-five years of it – enhancing the lives of millions of people around the world by doing what he loved. There was no question that he'd been born to do this *Gardeners' World* thing; he had inspired and touched so many people, knowing that the more they gardened the better their lives would be.

My biggest fear about visiting the funeral parlour was that it would leave me with an image of Dad that detracted from the man I'd known and loved but I needn't have worried. That daft grin just reinforced all that I knew about him!

His untimely death happened within a year of the conversation about his newly written Will. Uncle Tony and Lynda were in charge of the arrangements as they were his executors.

The church service in Exton went without incident. Dad's plot was in the far corner of the graveyard and it wasn't far to carry the coffin, but even so my heart started to pound. Neither Tony nor Lynda had mentioned any strange requests in the Will but I wasn't entirely sure that Dad had been joking about his send-off.

By the time I got to the graveside my mouth was dry with nerves. The pallbearers placed the coffin on wooden struts laid across the grave, slid the ropes under it and were ready to go. I wasn't listening the anything the vicar was saying but was focused on the coffin… I could picture Dad's grinning face when he was telling me of his plan.

The pallbearers grasped the ropes and raised the coffin from its position while one of them removed the wooden struts. The coffin hovered briefly above the hole and started its descent – the suspense was now unbearable.

When Dad's final journey began, the coffin slid perfectly into the hole all the way to the bottom with no assistance from the vicar. Phew! I know it's not the usual thought to have when your Dad's coffin has just reached its final destination but what popped into my head was: 'The old devil has done me again!'

He could find humour in almost anything, so why not in his own death? And the one thing I do know is that he was making sure that he had the last laugh!